Samuel French Acting Edition

CW00544762

Remember ~~My Name~~

A Story of Survival in Wartime France

by Joanna Halpert Kraus

SAMUELFRENCH.COM   SAMUELFRENCH.CO.UK

FOR PRODUCTION ENQUIRIES

UNITED STATES AND CANADA
Info@SamuelFrench.com
1-866-598-8449

UNITED KINGDOM AND EUROPE
Plays@SamuelFrench.co.uk
020-7255-4302

Each title is subject to availability from Samuel French, depending upon
country of performance. Please be aware that *REMEMBER MY NAME*
may not be licensed by Samuel French in your territory. Professional
and amateur producers should contact the nearest Samuel French
office or licensing partner to verify availability.

MUSIC USE NOTE

Licensees are solely responsible for obtaining formal written permission from copyright owners to use copyrighted music in the performance of this play and are strongly cautioned to do so. If no such permission is obtained by the licensee, then the licensee must use only original music that the licensee owns and controls. Licensees are solely responsible and liable for all music clearances and shall indemnify the copyright owners of the play(s) and their licensing agent, Samuel French, against any costs, expenses, losses and liabilities arising from the use of music by licensees. Please contact the appropriate music licensing authority in your territory for the rights to any incidental music.

IMPORTANT BILLING AND CREDIT REQUIREMENTS

If you have obtained performance rights to this title, please refer to your licensing agreement for important billing and credit requirements.

REMEMBER MY NAME, under the title of *THE DEVIL'S ORPHAN,* won first prize in the Third IUPUI National Playwriting Competition and was produced at Indiana University-Purdue University at Indianapolis, 1989.

The play was presented by the IUPUI Theatre under the direction of Dorothy L. Webb with the following designers: scene, J. Edgar Webb; lighting, Jack Douglas Sutton; costume, Brenda Rome Whitney; sound, A. Michelle Simmons; technical, Jack Douglas Sutton; and with the following cast:

RACHEL SIMON (aka MADELINE PETIT)........................
                                    Becka Vargus
PAULINE SIMON ....Jill Riesmeyer
LÉON SIMON ....Bob Vogel
MARIE-THÉRÈSE BARBIÈRE...........................Mary Flick
SUZANNE FLEURY.................................Kate Lawton
JULIAN DELACOUR.................................Paul Baker
GÉRARD LA SALLE ....Patrick Timbers
HANS SCHMIDT...Will Gould
YVETTE REYNAUD ....Sandra Hartlieb
PÈRE ANTOINE ....Tom Test

REMEMBER MY NAME, under the title of *THE DEVIL'S ORPHAN*, was subsequently presented by the Rochester Academy of Performing Arts, Diane Nuccitelli, producer and Marcy Gamzon, director, with set and light design by P. Gibson Ralph, with costumes by Lisa Shaw, and with the following cast:

RACHEL SIMON (aka MADELINE PETIT)
.... Danielle Bonadio
PAULINE SIMON.................................. Diane Davis
LÉON SIMON... Roger Gans
MARIE-THÉRÈSE BARBIÈRE.................. Sonya Raimi
SUZANNE FLEURY...............................Peggy Nakis
JULIAN DELACOUR.......................... Christopher Cline
GÉRARD LA SALLE............................. Dick Van Ness
HANS SCHMIDT.................................. Darryl Lance
YVETTE REYNAUD............................ Maxine Peters
PÈRE ANTOINE...................................... Jim Scholes

REMEMBER MY NAME was presented by the Jerusalem Group Theatre, Alan Jacobson, Producer; Shela Xoregos, Director, during June of 1992. The cast (in order of appearance):
PAULINE SIMON.............................. Ruth Bender
LÉON SIMON...................................... Alan Barr
RACHEL SIMON.....................................Orli Cotel
PÈRE ANTOINE .... Kerry Wolf
YVETTE REYNAUD ....Jane K. Hamilton
MARIE-THÉRÈSE BARBIÈRE................ Glen Lincoln
GÉRARD LA SALLE......................... Paul David Ross
SUZANNE FLEURY......................... Elizabeth Striker
HANS SCHMIDT...................................Pierre Lang
JULIEN DELACOUR ....Jonathan Freiman
VENDOR .... Ruth Bender
BRITISH RADIO VOICE......................... Bruce Wall
      Set Design: Murphy Gigliotti
      Lighting Design: David J. Lander
      Costume Design: Kenneth J. Wyrtch
      Sound Design: Kenn Dovel
      Stage Manager: Lori A. Brown
      Asst. Stage Manager: Kenn Sunshine

The characters in this play are fictional, as is the name of the small village, St. Laurent des Pins. However, the story is inspired by and based on historical accounts of the period.

Dedicated to Claude, to Le Chambon-Sur-Lignon, and to all those who had the courage to say "No."

CHARACTERS

RACHEL SIMON (aka MADELEINE PETIT) — A student. Resourceful, idealistic, and curious. About 10.

PAULINE SIMON — Her mother. Religious, family-centered, cautious. 32.

LÉON SIMON — Her father. A man of action. 37

MARIE-THÉRÈSE BARBIÈRE — A war widow, independent, proud. 60.

SUZANNE FLEURY — The village school teacher. Knowledgeable, attractive. Assists the Maquis. 26.

JULIEN DELACOUR — A leader in the Underground Resistance, the Maquis. By profession a journalist. Intense, impulsive. 30.

GÉRARD LA SALLE — A gendarme. Enforces the laws of France, no matter what they are. Sentimental. 55.

HANS SCHMIDT	A Nazi officer. Handsome, well-educated man of the world, who follows party policy assiduously. 35.
YVETTE REYNAUD	Madame Barbière's neighbor. An opportunist. 45.
PÈRE ANTOINE	A Jesuit priest. Follows his conscience. 55.
VENDOR	Non-speaking. Only hands and shadowy face seen. Can be played by PAULINE or LÉON.

TIME

The play takes place during World War II, 1942-1945.

THE PLACE

The action takes place in Southern and South Central France, in the Unoccupied Zone.

Scenic design can be minimal, a unit set with levels, selected set pieces and possible projections to suggest atmosphere and locale. What is vital is that the story flows freely, the action moves quickly, and the production is taut.

ACT I

Scene 1	A basement hotel room in Marseilles. November, 1942
Scene 2	A carriage in a French train. Two days later.
Scene 3	Madame Barbière's kitchen in St. Laurent des Pins. Immediately afterwards.
Scene 4	The village school. January, 1943.
Scene 5	The Town Hall. March, 1944
Scene 6	Madame Barbière's kitchen. June, 1944.

ACT II

ACT I

Scene 1

SCENE: A city street in Marseilles. The Unoccupied Zone of France. November, 1942.
The WHISTLE of a French train. School boys BEATING someone up.

RACHEL. (*Voice offstage.*) No! Leave me alone. Let me go. No-o!

(*SOUND: A GUN SHOT. The wailing of a French SIREN.*
RACHEL races on, fleeing a gang of school boys. SHE is resourceful, idealistic, and curious. But at present SHE is beaten up. Her uniform is torn and her face and knees are bleeding. SHE turns and realizes they're not pursuing her. RACHEL stops to collect herself, discovers injuries, wipes the blood from her face and puts a handkerchief around her bleeding knee. Stifling the tears, SHE continues running, halting only in the momentary safety of shadows.
RACHEL exits.
SOUND: The WHISTLE of a French train.

LIGHTING comes up on a basement hotel room in Marseilles.)

AT RISE: PAULINE is setting the table for supper. PAULINE SIMON is married to LÉON and is the mother of Rachel. She is religious, family-centered and cautious. 32.
LÉON peers out through a slit in the hotel curtain. LÉON SIMON is married to Pauline and the father of Rachel. He is a man of action. 37.
SOUND: GUNFIRE, followed by the wailing of a French SIREN.
PAULINE freezes.
Suddenly past the basement window, there are running feet. Then the THUDDING SOUND of heavy boots and the blare of a military BRASS BAND.
LÉON slumps in a chair.

PAULINE. What's happened?
LÉON. They're here. In Marseilles.
PAULINE. This is the Free Zone. That's why we came here. The French and German governments made a pact.
LÉON. A devil's pact. (*LÉON crosses to the desk, searching for papers.*)

(*PAULINE rushes to the window.*)

LÉON. Stay away from the window!!! PAULINE!!

PAULINE. Where's Rachel?

(RACHEL SIMON stands in the doorway.)

RACHEL. Maman.
PAULINE. *(Runs to her.)* RACHEL!
RACHEL. I don't have the bread, Maman. I don't have ... *(Bursts into tears in her mother's arms.)*
PAULINE. Léon, some clean rags and some hot water quickly.

(LÉON goes.)

PAULINE. Where were you?
RACHEL. Outside the cinema.
PAULINE. But that's nowhere near the bakery!
RACHEL. *(Between sobs.)* I wanted ... to find out ... what was playing. But I saw a big sign, "No Jews Allowed." Maman, it wasn't there yesterday.

(LÉON returns with rags. PAULINE begins to cleanse wounds.)

LÉON. Who was it? Who beat you up like this?
RACHEL. Some boys. A gang.
PAULINE. If you'd do what you're told and not be so headstrong! The cinema!
LÉON. Did you recognize any of them?

RACHEL. Some were from my school.

PAULINE. Your new school!

RACHEL. They had the same uniforms. But, Papa, they all had Nazi armbands. Except one. Brand new armbands. And one of them had a flag.

LÉON. The Nazis do a thorough job.

RACHEL. They started hitting me. One of them yelled, "Forget it. She's just a kid." But the one carrying the flag, said, "This'll teach her a lesson she won't forget."

LÉON. Why didn't you run?

RACHEL. I did. They came after me. The one with the flag yelled, "We'll get rid of your kind."

PAULINE. Rachel, are you hurt? Is anything broken?

RACHEL. Oh, Maman, it wasn't the sticks. They were laughing at me!

PAULINE. Léon, she is not going back to that school!

LÉON. (*Thoughtfully.*) No. No, she's not.

RACHEL. But I didn't cry, Papa. No matter how hard they hit me.

PAULINE. You can cry all you want now.

LÉON. How did you get home?

RACHEL. There was a gunshot. They turned to look. The boy without the armband whispered, "Run!" But, Maman, I forgot the bread.

LÉON. Never mind about the bread. (*Hugs her.*) Tonight we'll eat less.

RACHEL. Papa, why do they hate us so much? WHY?

LÉON. Because ... we are a little different. (*Shrugs.*) Because it's easy.

RACHEL. Easy?

LÉON. Easier to blame us than try to solve the problem. (*To Pauline wearily.*) That's our history, isn't it?

RACHEL. Papa, I was scared. Awful scared. But I didn't let them know. And I bit one of them, too. He yelled!

LÉON. (*Laughs.*) Next thing you know you'll be a French spy!

PAULINE. How can you laugh at a time like this?

LÉON. There are times, Pauline, when you can either laugh or cry. Léon Simon chooses to laugh. My one and only daughter is saved by the gunfire of the Nazi invasion. but just before that happened, she bit the enemy, and he howled like a baby. It's a story for her grandchildren.

RACHEL. (*Giggles.*) Papa, you make things seem all right. You make me laugh. You always do.

LÉON. It comes with the job of being papa. And right now that's the only job I have. The only job I have - worth keeping. (*LÉON goes to the drawer and takes out an official identify card and an ink pad.*) Rachel, put your thumb in this, and then press it on the square right here.

(*RACHEL does.*)

LÉON. Now say, "My name is Madeleine Petit."

RACHEL. (*Repeats.*) My name is Madeleine Petit. But why, Papa? My name's Rachel Simon. Who's Madeleine Petit?

(*SOUND: CLOCK striking five.*)

LÉON. As of five o'clock — you are!

RACHEL. But that's lying. You told me never to lie.

LÉON. The world' s just turned upside down. When it's right side up, we can live again — and stop lying. For now you must forget you were ever Rachel Simon.

PAULINE. NO!

RACHEL. Why, Papa? I don't want to forget.

LÉON. You must forget you are a brave and beautiful Jewish girl.

RACHEL. PAPA!

LÉON. Not that Madeleine isn't brave and beautiful. She is. Definitely. But she is not Jewish. And she has never heard of Léon and Pauline Simon.

PAULINE. Léon, we discussed this, and I said, "No." Only if it were an emergency.

LÉON. What do you call this? They've invaded Marseilles.

PAULINE. She's not ready.

LÉON. Ready? Who is ready? Do you think I want to do this? But alone she has a chance to survive.

RACHEL. Alone? ALONE! Maman?

PAULINE. Léon, she's only ten years old.

LÉON. With a whole life ahead of her! And I won't let those barbarians take it away!

PAULINE. (*Frantic.*) The family should stay together.

LÉON. The only way to survive is to separate.

RACHEL. Why can't we go together?

LÉON. Because, you're the only one who has the right papers. I am sending you to St. Laurent des Pins.

RACHEL. Where?

LÉON. A tiny village in the mountains. Snowed in all winter. A perfect place to hide.

RACHEL. But where is it?

LÉON. Auvergne.

RACHEL. I never heard of it.

LÉON. With a little luck the Nazis never heard of it either.

RACHEL. Do we have relatives there?

LÉON. No.

RACHEL. Friends?

LÉON. Madeleine Petit will make some.

RACHEL. Papa, Auvergne is so far away.

LÉON. Yes. Far from all this madness. That's why I'm sending you. Now here's your new papers: your identity card with photograph and thumb print, your birth certificate, a food ration card. You'll need these. Don't lose them. You're going to start a whole new life.

RACHEL. Papa, I can't.

LÉON. (*His gesture interrupts her.*) You don't know what you can do until you try. Now, this is the most important of all. Don't ever tell anyone that you had another name. Not even someone you think you can trust. NEVER!

RACHEL. Why not?

LÉON. (*Stern.*) Promise me!

RACHEL. All right, I promise, but why not, Papa?

LÉON. Because one slip of the tongue, and you're dead.

RACHEL. (*Scared.*) Papa, can't you and Maman come too? Please!

LÉON. It's safer this way.

RACHEL. How will I get there?

LÉON. By train.

PAULINE. They'll arrest her. Jews can't travel.

LÉON. No. But Madeleine Petit can. And she will. Three hundred and fifty kilometers. All the way from Marseilles to St. Laurent des Pins. (*To Rachel.*) Don't look so frightened. Above all, don't give them any cause for suspicion.

RACHEL. But I am frightened.

LÉON. Of course, you are! It's dangerous. Some people think when you're brave, you have no fear. No. To be brave means you don't *show* your fear.

PAULINE. Léon, she's just a child.

LÉON. Not any longer! Go change. Your bag is under the bed. Packed. The train's at eight. Hurry.

(*RACHEL exits.*)

PAULINE. She won't know what to do.

LÉON. She'll learn.

PAULINE. It isn't right.

LÉON. The whole war isn't right.

PAULINE. I only have one child.

LÉON. And I will do anything to save her!

PAULINE. What if something happens to her?

LÉON. Did you forget what happened to our neighbors in Paris? The reason we ran?

PAULINE. Why St. Laurent des Pins?

LÉON. I told you before. They'll never let a child go hungry.

PAULINE. (*Desperate.*) Léon, can't we decide this tomorrow?

LÉON. Tonight there's confusion. Easier for her to escape. And wait for what? They took our business. They took our home. They're not going to take our daughter.

PAULINE. There must be some other way.

(*SOUND: GUNFIRE and the wail of a French SIREN.*)

LÉON. Not now! (*Persuading her.*) In St. Laurent des Pins she'll lead an ordinary life.

PAULINE. Ordinary! Away from her own mother and father?

(*SOUND: Marching JACKBOOTS and ORDERS shouted in German.*)

LÉON. We are sending her away to live, Pauline. TO LIVE!

PAULINE. (*Looks at him shocked. Pause. Softly.*) All right. (*Deliberately.*) All right.

(*LÉON kisses Pauline.*)

PAULINE. Léon, I want her to remember the Sabbath.

LÉON. I'll get her. (*Exits.*)

(*PAULINE gets out three Sabbath candles on a tray, one for each member of the family, and a wine goblet. As the reality hits her, SHE loses control and cries. But quickly SHE straightens herself up. SHE lights the three candles, covers her head with a white shawl, closes her eyes, and waves her hands toward her three times in the traditional welcoming of the Sabbath blessing.*
RACHEL and LÉON enter.
PAULINE puts her hands before her face, closes her eyes and recites the Sabbath blessing.)

PAULINE.   (Translation)
(*Recites in* Blessed art Thou,
Hebrew.) the Eternal our God,
Ba-ruch a-ta, ha- King of the
shem E-lo-hei-nu, Universe, Who has
me-lech ha-o-lam, sanctified us with
a-sher kid-sha-nu His command-
b'mitz-votav ments and
ve-tsi-va-nu- le- enjoined us to
hud-lik-ner shel kindle the Sabbath
shal-bat. lights.

(*LÉON raises the wine goblet and says the traditional blessing.*)

LÉON.   (Translation)
(*Recites in* Blessed is the Lord
Hebrew.) our God, Ruler of
Ba-ruch a-ta, ha- the Universe,
shem E-lo-hei-nu, Creator of the fruit
me-lech ha-o-lam, of the vine.
bo-rei pe-ri ha-go-
fen.

(*LÉON sips the wine. PAULINE and RACHEL each take a sip from the same goblet.*

PAULINE. We'll have to imagine the Sabbath loaf is in front of us.

LEON,	(Translation)

LEON,
PAULINE, and
RACHEL. *(Recite
in Hebrew.)*

Ba-ruch a-ta, ha-
shem E-lo-hei-nu,
me-lech ha-o-lam,
ha-mo-tzi le-chem
min-ha-a-retz

Blessed art Thou,
the Eternal our God,
King of the
Universe, who
brings forth bread
from the earth.

*(PAULINE mimes taking a piece of the Sabbath
loaf and hands the tray to LÉON and
RACHEL who each mime taking a chunk.)*

PAULINE. *(Kisses Léon and Rachel.)* Good
Shabbas.
LÉON. Good Shabbas.
RACHEL. Good Shabbas.
RACHEL. Maman, where's the lace
tablecloth?
PAULINE. Rented rooms cost money.
RACHEL. *(Horrified.)* You sold it!

(PAULINE nods upset.)

RACHEL. You said you'd never do that. No
matter what happened.

(PAULINE looks at Léon unable to respond.)

LÉON. Things are replaceable. Lives are not! (*Gestures to soup tureen.*) She's got to hurry.

(*THEY sit down to their meager supper. PAULINE ladles out soup.*
LIGHTING: The street is now dark.
As they eat. RACHEL looks out the window nervously trying to gather courage. THEY eat a few spoonfuls in silence.)

RACHEL. I've never been out alone after dark.

PAULINE. I never let you!

RACHEL. When will—

LÉON. (*Interrupts.*) When the war's over. But stay in St. Laurent des Pins. (*A lighter tone.*) I don't want to have to hunt all over France for you!

RACHEL. What do I do first?

PAULINE. You see!

LÉON. A sensible question! Just what I'd expect from Madeleine Petit. The directions are easy. Finding a home will be harder. As soon as you arrive go to the village priest or the school teacher.

RACHEL. What do I tell them?

LÉON. Don't mention Paris. Just say that you've come from Marseilles.

RACHEL. I have.

LÉON. Tell them that when the Nazis invaded, you lost your home.

RACHEL. We did.

LÉON. And that your parents were deported for forced labor.

PAULINE. Léon!

LÉON. (*To Pauline.*) She has to know! Marseilles was safe until today. Tomorrow it could be Paris all over again. (*To Rachel.*) Say you need a place to stay, and you'll work hard in exchange. A farm can always use extra hands.

RACHEL. It won't be long, will it, Papa? Will it?

(*SOUND: roar of MOTORCYCLES, tramp of soldiers' JACKBOOTS. LÉON can't answer. PAULINE embraces her.*)

PAULINE. My dearest, as soon as the first star appears, say goodnight; and I'll say goodnight too. For as long as we're apart.

RACHEL. Oh, Maman. Like letters. Our own special letters.

PAULINE. Be a good girl. Remember all I've taught you. But most of all, remember that I love you. (*Covering her emotions.*) You'll need your winter coat. I'll get it. (*Exits.*)

LÉON. You know the way to La Gare Saint Charles. You pass it every day.

RACHEL. Can't you go with me? Just that far?

LÉON. No. If they stopped us for an identity check, none of us would get through. Maman and I have to ... arrange ... for new papers ... Remember how we used to make up stories?

(*RACHEL nods.*)

LÉON. This one you must always tell the same way. Ready?
RACHEL. Ready.
LÉON. Name?
RACHEL. Madeleine Petit.
LÉON. Occupation?
RACHEL. Uh ... uh ... student.
LÉON. Good. Which school?
RACHEL. Elementary school.
LÉON. Where are you going?
RACHEL. St. Laurent des Pins.
LÉON. Why?
RACHEL. Uh ... uh ... to see ... uh ... my relatives.
LÉON. Good. But don't hesitate. (*With a feigned kindly tone.*) Now what's your real name?

(*PAULINE returns with coat and beret.*)

RACHEL. (*Slips.*) Rachel Simon.
LÉON. (*Slaps her face.*) NO!!!
RACHEL. PAPA!
PAULINE. LÉON! How could you?
LÉON. You don't think the Nazis will do worse? This is a game of life and death. One mistake - and it's over. (*To Rachel.*) Let's try again. Your name is?

RACHEL. (*Sniffling.*) Madeleine.

LÉON. (*Shakes her roughly.*) Madeleine what?

RACHEL. MADELEINE PETIT!

LÉON. Good! Say it again.

RACHEL. Madeleine Petit.

LÉON. Say it over and over. Until it's second nature.

RACHEL. (*Muttering.*) Madeleine Petit. Madeleine Petit. Madeleine Petit.

LÉON. Good. Good. Now I'm going to give you some money. I wish it were more. But it'll get you there. Are you ready?

RACHEL. (*Scared.*) So soon? What time is it?

(*Peeks in his vest pocket, an old familiar gesture.*)

RACHEL. Papa, where's your watch?

LÉON. (*Picks up identity papers.*) Here! Genuine forged false identity papers. The best in the black market. And here. The money for your train ticket. It was a good watch. It fetched a good price. (*Hands envelope to her.*)

RACHEL. Oh, Papa, you loved that pocket watch. It was Grand-père's.

LÉON. Yes. (*Hugs Rachel tightly.*) But I love my daughter more!

RACHEL. (*Crosses to Pauline and THEY hug goodbye.*) Maman!

(*PAULINE gives her coat, which RACHEL puts on.*)

LÉON. (*Shows directions on envelope.*) Here's the numbers of the trains. From Marseilles you take one train direct to St. George d'Aurac. You'll have to change trains there for Le Puy. From Le Puy, it's only about twenty kilometers to St. Laurent des Pins. (*Looks out the window.*) Better go out the back way. Wait until the street is empty. Make sure no one follows you. Go straight to the station. When you've bought your ticket get on the train immediately. Don't talk to anyone. I'm counting on you, Madeleine Petit!

RACHEL. (*Crosses to Pauline, scared.*) Adieu, Maman.

PAULINE. (*Quickly.*) No, no, not adieu. Adieu means goodbye forever. Au revoir means till we see you again. And we will see you again. I promise. (*Kisses Rachel tenderly.*) Au revoir, my darling.

(*RACHEL picks up suitcase. LÉON and PAULINE cross with her to hotel door.*)

LÉON. Au revoir, Madeleine.

RACHEL. (*Turns for one last look at her parents.*) Au revoir. (*Exits.*)

(*PAULINE turns to Léon crying. HE holds her in his arms. LIGHTING fades.*)

End of ACT I, Scene 1

ACT I

Scene 2

SCENE: A carriage in a French train bound for the Haute-Loire region in Auvergne in South Central France. Two days later.
RACHEL sits stiffly in the carriage.

AT RISE: PÈRE ANTOINE, a Jesuit priest, a man who follows his conscience, 55, sits reading a book.
YVETTE REYNAUD, an opportunist, 45, is dozing.

SOUND: The TRAIN stops abruptly.

YVETTE. (*Wakes up with a start.*) Where are we?
PÈRE ANTOINE. (*Peering out the window.*) Just outside the station. Le Puy. (*Still peering.*) There's some sort of trouble.
YVETTE. (*Sighs.*) That's all there is these days.

(*SOUND: VOICES shouting.*)

YVETTE. I can't make it out. It's all in German. What are all those soldiers doing?

PÈRE ANTOINE. Chasing someone.

YVETTE. Oh, I see him! I see him! (*Calls out window.*) Over there! (*Pause.*) The horse just knocked down the flower cart!

(*SOUND: A GUNSHOT. RACHEL screams and buries her head. PÈRE ANTOINE immediately tries to calm her.*)

YVETTE. Must they do such things in public! Scaring women half to death.

PÈRE ANTOINE. My God! They've just left the man. Beside the tracks!

YVETTE. Who was it?

PÈRE ANTOINE. (*Shakes his head.*) A poor Jew trying to escape.

(PÈRE ANTOINE quietly recites a prayer in Latin from the liturgy of Good Friday under Yvette's next speech. [See production note.])

Ego eduxi te de
    Aeypto
Demerso Pharone
    in Mare
    Rubrum, et tu
    me tradidisti
Principibus
    sacerdotum.
Ego ante te aperui
    mare,
Et tu apereruisti
    lancea
Latus meum.
Ego ante te praeivi
    in columna
    nubis,
Et tu me duxisti and
    Praetorium
    Pilatis.
Ego te pavi manna
    per desertum,
Et tu me cecidisti
a lapis et fiagellis.

I led you out of the
    land of Egypt
Destroyed Pharoah
    in the Red Sea,
    and you handed
    me over
To the authorities of
    the Church
I opened the sea
    before you,
And you have
    opened my side
    with a lance
I went before you in
    a pillar of
    cloud,
And you led me to
    the Tribunal of
    Pilate.
I fed you with
    manna in the
    desert
And you have
    struck me down
    with slaps and
    scourging.

Ego dedi tibi sceptrum regale, Et tu dedisti capiti meo spineam coronam. Ego te exaltavi magna virtute, Et tu me suspendisti, In patibulo Crucis.	I gave you a royal sceptre, And you gave my head A crown of thorns. I raised you up in great power, And you have suspended me On the gibbet of the cross.

YVETTE. He must have been a criminal! (*Grabs newspaper, searching.*) Why ... did you know? There's a five hundred franc reward for turning in a Jew! Right here. Look. On page two. And I saw him. Five hundred francs! I could have fed my whole family for a month! (*SOUND: The TRAIN starts to move again.*) All this stopping and starting. Next time my sister's sick, she can come and visit me.

(*PÈRE ANTOINE finishes prayer.*)

YVETTE. Père Antoine, you know I never pry; but why on earth did you say a prayer for him? Someone who doesn't even go to our church? And a criminal?

PÈRE ANTOINE. My dear Madame Reynaud, perhaps the differences down here don't seem as important up there!

GÉRARD. (*Calling offstage.*) Papers! All identification papers. Please, have your papers ready!

(*GÉRARD LA SALLE enters. He is a gendarme, who enforces the laws of France, no matter what they are. Sentimental, 55. GÉRARD checks Yvette's papers.*)

GÉRARD. Yvette Reynaud. Ah, but you look younger than your photograph, madame.

YVETTE. (*Pleased.*) Oh, monsieur. Well, it's a wonder I do. Tending an ill sister all week.

GÉRARD. You'll soon be home, now. (*GÉRARD inspects Père Antoine's photograph closely.*)

PÈRE ANTOINE. (*Laughs.*) I can see you notice the difference. I'm thinner now. Before the war I ate better.

GÉRARD. We all did. These are hard times. Thank you, Père Antoine.

(*PÈRE ANTOINE resumes reading. GÉRARD crosses to Rachel.*)

GÉRARD. Hello, there, young lady. And what is your name?

(*RACHEL opens her mouth to speak and no sound comes out. Mutely she hands her papers over.*)

GÉRARD. Madeleine Petit. (*Looks sharply at her.*) Don't you know your own name?

(*RACHEL nods.*)

GÉRARD. (*Shakes his head disapprovingly.*) Such times! I certainly wouldn't let my young daughter travel alone. Where are you going?
RACHEL. To ... to ... visit ... relatives.
GÉRARD. Let's see your train ticket.

(*RACHEL hands it to him.*)

GÉRARD. St. Laurent. That's the next stop. (*Scrutinizing papers.*) Ah, from Marseilles. I know it well. The best fish on the Mediterranean. (*Kisses his fingers.*) Ah, Père Antoine, what I wouldn't give for some bouillabaisse à la Marseillaise!

(*PÈRE ANTOINE nods in agreement.*)

GÉRARD. (*To Rachel.*) Is someone meeting you in St. Laurent des Pins?

(*RACHEL hesitates.*)

PÈRE ANTOINE. (*Takes him aside.*) Officer, can't you see the child is upset? She saw what happened.

YVETTE. It was practically under this carriage window. Almost like ... the movies!

GÉRARD. Ah! Ah, Père Antoine, something like that's happened every day this week. After awhile you get used to it. They try to run away. Our job is to stop them.

PÈRE ANTOINE. What kind of job is that for a decent Frenchman?

GÉRARD. We stop them ... if we see them. Me? I never see them.

PÈRE ANTOINE. Officer, I was so absorbed in my book, I wasn't paying attention. The child is travelling with me.

YVETTE. She is!

GÉRARD. Well, well, why didn't you say so? Sorry, Father. (*Checks papers.*) Regulations. You understand.

PÈRE ANTOINE. Certainly. But she's very tired. It's a long way from Marseilles, officer— and good bouillabaisse!

GÉRARD. Ah, Père Antoine, for a man who loves fish, as I do, to work in Auvergne .. is purgatory! (*Catches himself.*) I hope I didn't offend you, Father.

PÈRE ANTOINE. (*Laughs.*) Not at all. Not at all. (*To Rachel.*) Rest now, Madeleine. I'll wake you, when we get there.

(*RACHEL pretends to sleep.*)

GÉRARD. Why is she going to St. Laurent des Pins?

PÈRE ANTOINE. If I had my way, officer, I'd take all the children out of the city. War's no place for a child.

GÉRARD. (*Agreeing.*) No. (*Hands papers to Père Antoine.*) Here. Let her sleep. We have to check the papers on all the trains. Just following orders.

PÈRE ANTOINE. So am I.

GÉRARD. (*Exiting.*) Papers. All identification papers.

YVETTE. Such a quiet little thing. I had no idea that she was with you, Père Antoine. Why, she hasn't spoken the whole way to you.

PÈRE ANTOINE. Or to anyone else. She's well brought up. (*Pointedly.*) She knows better than to chatter, when I'm trying to prepare a Sunday sermon.

YVETTE. Oh! (*Pause.*) Then, is she a relative of yours?

PÈRE ANTOINE. In a way.

YVETTE. Oh, you people from Auvergne! You never ever talk. It's maddening. Where I come from in the south, we practice the art of conversation. But you Auvergnats, you hardly ever open your mouths. It must be the climate. Why my husband's family ...

(*SOUND: TRAIN lurches to a stop.*)

PÈRE ANTOINE. Ah, here we are! Permit me to help you with your baggage, Madame Reynaud.

YVETTE. Why, thank you. Thank you, Père Antoine.

(*PÈRE ANTOINE opens carriage door and puts Yvette's luggage out.*)

YVETTE. But why didn't you introduce us, when I got on at Nimes? Now, I know all about little girls. I raised six of them. So be sure to ...

PÈRE ANTOINE. (*Assisting Yvette out.*) Thank you, Madame Reynaud.

(*YVETTE exits.*)

PÈRE ANTOINE. Madeleine. Madeleine, we're here.

RACHEL. I'm awake. Why did you lie?

PÈRE ANTOINE. Lie? I didn't lie.

RACHEL. You said I was with you.

PÈRE ANTOINE. You are. I vowed to look after any child who's in need. But I didn't introduce myself. I'm Père Antoine from St. Laurent des Pins.

RACHEL. I'm Madeleine Petit.

PÈRE ANTOINE. Yes. But when the police officer asked you, you forgot.

RACHEL. No! No, I just lost my voice.

PÈRE ANTOINE. Madeleine, your name must be comfortable—like an old shoe. Particularly, if the name is new.

RACHEL. (*Stiffens.*) How do you know?

PÈRE ANTOINE. I don't! And what I don't know, I can't tell! Remember that.

RACHEL. You saved my life just now.

PÈRE ANTOINE. (*Lifts suitcase down and takes her hand. Casually.*) Just following orders.

(*PÈRE ANTOINE and RACHEL exit through carriage door.*)

End of ACT I, Scene 2

ACT I

Scene 3

SCENE: Immediately afterwards. The traditional kitchen-room of Mme. Barbière's stone farm house. There is a black cast iron stove with iron cooking pots and utensils hanging above it. There are fresh lace curtains at the windows and framed ornamental patterns of lace hanging on the wall.

*AT RISE: MARIE-THÉRÈSE BARBIÈRE is
making lace, peering through her glasses at
the netlike fabric of thread. SHE is a war
widow, independent, proud, 60. SHE wears
mourning black continually, and her white
hair is pulled off her face in a bun. Over her
somber attire is an apron that she rarely
removes, as SHE is always hard at work.*

PÈRE ANTOINE watches.

MARIE-THÉRÈSE. ... and they'd hung their
Nazi flag in front of the Town Hall. The mayor
stood there, tears in his eyes. But he could do
nothing. Nothing. Then the regiment marched on
to Le Puy. Ah, Père Antoine, what will happen to
us now? Now, that they're here.
PÈRE ANTOINE. I don't know. In Paris
meat's practically disappeared. The bread ration
would barely keep a sparrow alive. Women are
crying in the streets, because they can't feed their
children.
MARIE-THÉRÈSE. Savages! What they
can't kill, they starve! Well, they won't starve the
Auvergnats! We can make a cabbage grow from a
stone. (*Inviting him.*) I have some hot soup on the
stove.
PÈRE ANTOINE. Thank you. Not now. I
don't think they'll bother us. We're a poor
mountain village. There's nothing to steal.

MARIE-THÉRÈSE. Except our five-month winter. And we'll give them that!

(*THEY laugh.* MARIE-THÉRÈSE holds her lace up to the light and deftly corrects a stitch.)

PÈRE ANTOINE. Madame Barbière, your lace is the finest in St. Laurent des Pins.

MARIE-THÉRÈSE. Thank you, Père Antoine. My lace is my company, since Henri died. (*Looks at him sharply.*) But whenever you compliment me there's a favor not far behind. Have I ever refused? What is it?

PÈRE ANTOINE. This is different.

MARIE-THÉRÈSE. What?

PÈRE ANTOINE. A child.

MARIE-THÉRÈSE. What kind of child?

PÈRE ANTOINE. Intelligent. Polite. They lost their home to the Nazis.

MARIE-THÉRÈSE. Her parents?

PÈRE ANTOINE. Deported.

MARIE-THÉRÈSE. Such times! French!

PÈRE ANTOINE. French!

MARIE-THÉRÈSE. An orphan?

PÈRE ANTOINE. (*Carefully.*) Alone.

MARIE-THÉRÈSE. Ah! Ah, no, Père Antoine. It is too dangerous!

PÈRE ANTOINE. She has papers. All in order.

MARIE-THÉRÈSE. Did you see them?

PÈRE ANTOINE. Yes. She boarded the train at Marseilles. She stared out the window for hours. In utter silence. I've never seen anyone look so forlorn. Then at Le Puy the Nazis killed a man, and she screamed.

MARIE-THÉRÈSE. Naturally!

PÈRE ANTOINE. When the gendarme came though, she couldn't speak. She needs a home.

MARIE-THÉRÈSE. Père Antoine, you can't hide her here. If she's caught, we'll both be shot. The way they killed my husband.

PÈRE ANTOINE. Henri was a brave soldier, Madame Barbière. Very brave.

MARIE-THÉRÈSE. I don't want any more trouble.

PÈRE ANTOINE. I understand. (*Picks up his hat casually.*) I thought she might be company.

MARIE-THÉRÈSE. My neighbor across the field, Madame Reynaud looks in on me, even when the snow is knee deep. So how could I hide her with that one poking her nose into my cabbage soup every day?

PÈRE ANTOINE. Madame Reynaud! She was on the same train. I said Madeleine was with me.

MARIE-THÉRÈSE. Madeleine?

PÈRE ANTOINE. The child.

MARIE-THÉRÈSE. Where is she now?

PÈRE ANTOINE. Outside. (*Crosses to window.*)

MARIE-THÉRÈSE. Outside! Good Lord! Outside in the cold! Père Antoine, what were you thinking of? (*Crosses beside him.*)

(*PÈRE ANTOINE points out the window.*)

MARIE-THÉRÈSE. She looks half frozen. You didn't say she was so little! Poor child so young to be alone in the world. Bring her in to sit by the stove, Père Antoine. At least she can get warm and have some hot soup. How could you leave a little child like that out in the cold? Bring her in here at once!

PÈRE ANTOINE. (*Suppressing a smile.*) Certainly, Madame Barbière.

(*PÈRE ANTOINE exits.*)

(MARIE-THÉRÈSE rustles about the stove and stirs pot.)

(*PÈRE ANTOINE enters with RACHEL.*)

PÈRE ANTOINE. Madame Barbière, this is Madeleine Petit. Madeleine, this is Madame Barbière.

RACHEL. (*Shyly.*) Hello, Madame Barbière.

MARIE-THÉRÈSE. (*Warmly.*) Come in, Madeleine.

(*MARIE-THÉRÈSE takes Rachel's coat.
RACHEL shivers. MARIE-THÉRÈSE looks
at Père Antoine disapprovingly.*)

MARIE-THÉRÈSE. Sit by the stove and get
warm. (*Puts coat near stove.*) This is ice cold!
Where are you from Madeleine?
RACHEL. Marseilles.
MARIE-THÉRÈSE. No wonder you're
shivering. It's always summer there, isn't it?
RACHEL. (*Agreeably.*) Yes, madame.
(*Shivers again.*)
MARIE-THÉRÈSE. Here, have some hot
soup.
RACHEL. Thank you, Madame Barbière.

(*RACHEL eats hungrily. Her manners
disappear, and SHE gulps soup. MARIE-
THÉRÈSE and PÈRE ANTOINE exchange
glances. RACHEL stops embarrassed by her
appetite.*)

RACHEL. This is wonderful soup.

MARIE-THÉRÈSE. (*Laughs.*) Hunger is the
best seasoning, little one. But we are are famous
in St. Laurent des Pins for our cabbage soup.
PÈRE ANTOINE. And our lace.

(*RACHEL looks up at framed lace. Puts bowl
down and goes to look more closely.*)

RACHEL. Oh-h-h-. Each one's different! Oh,
Madame Barbière ...

(*RACHEL stops in front of one particular piece.*)

RACHEL. I like that one!
MARIE-THÉRÈSE. (*Softly.*) That's my
favorite too. It's my own design. Do you think it
would make a nice wedding dress?
RACHEL. Oh, yes!! Is it very difficult to
make lace?
MARIE-THÉRÈSE. Come here. (*Shows
Rachel how to do a stitch.*) Lace making requires
sharp eyes, careful fingers, and patience. And
while you work on each tiny piece you have to see
the whole design in your head.
RACHEL. We had a lace tablecloth ... once. It
was for Sh ... holidays. Maman said one day,
when I got married, it would be mine. But ... but
... but now, it's gone.
MARIE-THÉRÈSE. (*Briskly.*) Well, then
you must make your own. Just like the girls do
here. They all have lace trousseaus. Madeleine,
how old are you now?
RACHEL. Ten.
MARIE-THÉRÈSE. Well then, there's plenty
of time before you get married! Plenty of time.
(*Spontaneously takes Rachel's small hand.*) Oh,
your hands are so cold! (*Rubs them.*) There! You
need wool mittens when you go out in weather like

this. (*Looks down.*) And wool socks. Madeleine, do you know how to knit!

RACHEL. No, Madame Barbière.

MARIE-THÉRÈSE. Good heavens! What do they teach at school these days?

RACHEL. I was learning French, history, geography, arithmetic, science, art and music. Oh, and sewing, too.

MARIE-THÉRÈSE. Sewing. Now, that's something useful.

RACHEL. I was at the top of my class, too. I was even learning English.

MARIE-THÉRÈSE. English? Sometimes at night we can pick up the British broadcast on the radio. (*To Père Antoine.*) Now, the Nazis arrest you for listening. They don't want us to hear the *real* news! But I say no one is going to tell me what to do in my own house, in front of my own fire. No one.

PÈRE ANTOINE. It's getting dark, Madame Barbière. We'd better be on our way.

MARIE-THÉRÈSE. It gets dark so early these days. (*Looks out the window.*) It's starting to snow. (*Goes to get Rachel's coat.*) And her coat's not even warm, yet. And she has no mittens.

PÈRE ANTOINE. But in an hour the roads will be too slippery.

MARIE-THÉRÈSE. Madeleine, someone must have sent you to St. Laurent des Pins. Who? Why?

PÈRE ANTOINE. Madame Barbière, the best kept secrets are the ones we don't know.

(*Pause.*)

MARIE-THÉRÈSE. That's true. Madeleine, I'd like to help you, but I can't. If the Nazis pound on the door, and they find you curled in a closet, that will be the end of both of us.

RACHEL. (*Rises.*) Thank you for the hot soup, madame. (*Puts her coat on. Crosses to door.*)

MARIE-THÉRÈSE. Not so fast! Not so fast! Where will she go tonight, Père Antoine?

PÈRE ANTOINE. I'll think of something. The Lord provides. Come, Madeleine.

MARIE-THÉRÈSE. The Lord has more sense than to be out in a St. Laurent blizzard. Wait a minute. Let me think. When it snows here, Madeleine, it can be up to your waist in no time. But that can keep the soldiers away as well. (*Thinking of a plan.*) I can't hide her, Père Antoine, ... but ... you say she has papers?

PÈRE ANTOINE. Yes. The gendarme inspected them. A food ration card too.

MARIE-THÉRÈSE. Hmm. We'd need that if...

(*PÈRE ANTOINE and RACHEL look at one another.*)

RACHEL. Oh, Madame Barbière, I wouldn't be any trouble, I promise! I'd be so quiet, you wouldn't even know I was here.

MARIE-THÉRÈSE. No, no, no, little one. A child should laugh. A child should sing. We were never blessed with a child. But there's a time in life, for everything. Père Antoine, I can't hide her but .... but ... my husband's cousin could come to visit, couldn't she? And she could go to school with the other girls, couldn't she? And in the evening she could learn to make lace.

RACHEL. Oh, yes, madame, yes! And I could wash the dishes and run to the bakery for you and ... and ... (*Hides tears.*)

MARIE-THÉRÈSE. (*Gently puts an arm around Rachel.*) She can't leave without warm clothes, and that's that. Not with winter on its way. She needs warm wool mittens and socks ... and a scarf. And she's not leaving till she has them. But, Madeleine, you'll have to knit them yourself!

RACHEL. (*Crushed.*) But I don't know how to knit!

MARIE-THÉRÈSE. I will teach you, little one. I will teach you.

PÈRE ANTOINE. Madame Barbière, just how long do you think it will take to make all those clothes?

MARIE-THÉRÈSE. Oh, that's hard to say, Père Antoine. Hard to say. It could take ...

awhile. (*Removes Rachel's beret.*) It could take ...
till the end of the war.

End of ACT I, Scene 3

ACT I

Scene 4

*SCENE: The village school for girls, January,
1943.*

*AT RISE: SUZANNE FLEURY is examining
Rachel's schoolwork. SUZANNE FLEURY is
the village school teacher, knowledgeable,
attractive, 26. RACHEL is in her seat, waiting
nervously.*

SUZANNE. Excellent, Madeleine. You've
done well in French grammar and in geography.
Not as well in mathematics. So, I have assigned
these extra pages. Bring them in tomorrow.
However, we are happy to have you in the school. I
hope you will continue to work hard and be an
honor student.
     RACHEL. Oh, yes! Oh, thank you. I will try,
Mademoiselle Fleury.

SUZANNE. I'm sure you will. Madeleine ... you said once that you studied English. Can you speak it?

RACHEL. Only a little. My last teacher liked Shakespeare. She used to read to us, and then we had to read aloud to her.

SUZANNE. Good practice. Now, you are excused, Madeleine. I must prepare tomorrow's lessons.

RACHEL. Goodbye, Mademoiselle Fleury.

SUZANNE. See you tomorrow, Madeleine.

(RACHEL exits with school bag. SUZANNE continues working.

HANS SCHMIDT enters. He is a Nazi officer, a handsome, well-educated man of the world, who follows party policy assiduously. 35. He is not a caricature villain.)

HANS. I see you work late, fräulein.

SUZANNE. (Startled.) It is customary to knock before you enter!

HANS. I must examine a list of your students, your textbooks, your lessons, and your exams.

SUZANNE. There are several plants in the room. Would you like to examine those as well!

HANS. This is no joking matter, fräulein. I advise you not to be frivolous. In Belgium we found stacks of false identity and ration cards in the headmaster's desk. (Opens hers and goes through contents.)

SUZANNE. What happened?

HANS. Some desks, you know, have false bottoms, but I know how to discover them. (*Continues his inspection.*) Before I was promoted to be an officer in the Führer's army, I was a cabinet maker. I know desks. (*HANS crosses and knocks on wall.*) And I know walls. Particularly hollow walls. Where someone may be hiding. (*Smiles at Suzanne.*) What happened? We shot him. Enemies, fräulein, can be anywhere.

SUZANNE. You are free to search the room. But I must get on with my work.

HANS. (*Places whip across her book.*) First you will answer my question, fräulein. It is a mistake to ignore me. You will give me the names of all Jewish students.

SUZANNE. What? What are you talking about?

HANS. Are there Jewish children in your school?

SUZANNE. (*Rises.*) We have only French children here! You must have something better to do than to storm into a village schoolhouse. Now, please leave.

HANS. Hand over the list.

SUZANNE. What list?

HANS. The list of names. Your student's names. The list. The list!

(*SUZANNE hands it over. HANS checks it
against his list.*)

HANS. Um-hm. Um-hm. Hm-m. Why is this
name not on my list?

SUZANNE. (*Looks.*) Oh, that's Madeleine.
She came after the term started. She's a relative of
the widow Barbière.

HANS. (*Checks his notes.*) Whose husband
was a prisoner of war until ... approximately a
year ago, when unfortunately he refused to
cooperate.

SUZANNE. (*A growing apprehension.*) I
don't know any of the details.

HANS. And you, you are Suzanne Fleury, a
graduate of La Sorbonne, a teacher at the village
school in St. Laurent des Pins, a former resident
of Le Puy, but who on December 7th went to board
with the widow Barbière. Why?

SUZANNE. How do you know all this?

HANS. The Kommondant is particular. Now,
you will answer the question. Why did you move
out after our soldiers took Le Puy? What are you
hiding?

SUZANNE. (*Laughs.*) Hiding? You don't
understand.

HANS. I warn you, fräulein, if you laugh at a
German officer the results may not be so funny.

SUZANNE. Surely in your country, people
laugh, monsieur—?

HANS. Herr Leutnant Schmidt. (*A broad smile crosses his face.*) We do laugh, fräulein. Personally, I like a good time. But you should never laugh at an officer.

SUZANNE. I'm not laughing at you, Herr Leutnant Schmidt.

HANS. No?

SUZANNE. Of course not. But it's clear you don't know the Haute Loire section of Auvergne. You ask what I'm hiding? Look out the window.

HANS. Snow! Again!

SUZANNE. Yes, Herr Leutnant Schmidt. Again and again and again. From November until May. And when the winds start, some of the mountain roads become impassable. That is why, when winter comes, I board in the village. From the look of that sky, I advise you to leave at once. The snow here falls fast.

HANS. I will return, fräulein. Have your books, your lessons, and your exams ready for inspection.

SUZANNE. When will that be?

HANS. Soon, fräulein. Very soon.

SUZANNE. I sincerely hope you will knock next time, Herr Leutnant Schmidt, and not surprise a lady!

HANS. (*Drawn to Suzanne.*) You are young, spirited, I like that. If you cooperate, I will see to it you have a real school to teach in ... in our New World.

SUZANNE. I already have a school to teach in ... in this world!

HANS. This! This is nothing! A country schoolhouse filled with French peasants.

SUZANNE. Then why waste your time here?

HANS. We will see each other again, fräulein. But next time ... (*A slight smile.*) I will knock first.

(*SUZANNE gathers her belongings, puts on her boots. SOUND: KNOCK at the door. SUZANNE hesitantly opens it. JULIEN DELACOUR enters quickly. He is a leader in the Underground Resistance Movement, the Maquis. By profession a journalist. Intense, impulsive, 30.*)

JULIEN. Mademoiselle Fleury?

SUZANNE. Yes. (*Glances out at snow.*) Can this wait until tomorrow?

JULIEN. No. No, it can't. (*Looks at her carefully.*) You don't recognize me, do you?

SUZANNE. No, monsieur ...

JULIEN. I'm Julien Delacour. We were in the same philosophy class. La Sorbonne.

SUZANNE. Oh? Did we meet?

JULIEN. No, not officially. I sat three rows behind you. When I finally had the courage to say hello, it was too late.

SUZANNE. Too late?

JULIEN. It was the day the Nazis took over the university. The Gestapo came in and knocked the professor to the floor.

SUZANNE. I remember. But when he got up, he said-

JULIEN. "Do not forget what you just saw. A man can be knocked down - and stand up again. And so can a country!"

SUZANNE. The end of our education.

JULIEN. Or the beginning! Suzanne ... may I call you Suzanne?

SUZANNE. Yes.

JULIEN. Suzanne, there are those of us who think the professor was right. We don't want to sit and wait for the Allies to rescue us.

SUZANNE. We can't wait! The Allies are still in North Africa.

JULIEN. We live here, and we must fight here. On our own soil. For our own country.

SUZANNE. A French underground?

JULIEN. Here in Auvergne, in St. Laurent des Pins, the Maquis will be born. We want this schoolhouse for a meeting.

SUZANNE. It's yours.

JULIEN. We need secrecy.

SUZANNE. We need success, Monsieur Delacour! The French are like puppets, obeying absurdities, ignoring atrocities. It has to stop!

JULIEN. (*Impulsively JULIEN hugs her, then backs off embarrassed.*) Suzanne, you are the spirit the Maquis needs!

SUZANNE. (*Laughs lightly.*) Tell me, what can I do?

JULIEN. Leave the door open.

SUZANNE. That's all?

JULIEN. For now! The Maquis meets here tonight. Tomorrow we go into action. Oh, I'll meet you at the cafe. Five o'clock?

SUZANNE. Five o'clock!

End of ACT I, Scene 4

ACT I

Scene 5

SCENE: The Town Hall. March, 1944, 15 months later.

AT RISE: HANS SCHMIDT is interrogating Rachel.

HANS. Now, tell the truth.

RACHEL. I've told you.

HANS. I don't believe you. It's a crime to help a prisoner.

RACHEL. All I did was mail a letter.

HANS. What secret information was inside?

RACHEL. It was a birthday card for his little girl.

HANS. Idiot! Where would a prisoner get a birthday card?

RACHEL. He made it. From scraps.

HANS. Again. Where did you and the prisoner meet?

RACHEL. I've told you. I was on my way home from school, and he was sweeping the snow from the Town Hall steps. He just asked me if I'd mail this letter for him, because he wasn't allowed to leave.

HANS. Then you admit you spoke to him!

RACHEL. Yes.

HANS. That alone is a crime! (*Checks his watch.*) Now, Madeleine, you've been here for three hours. Aren't you getting tired?

RACHEL. Yes.

HANS. Then identify the prisoner, I'll give you your coat and let you go home! (*Bribing her.*) If you're a good girl, I'll even give you some real chocolate.

RACHEL. Chocolate? But there's no chocolate in France anymore. I know that.

HANS. Ah, you're wrong. (*Opens his desk and holds out a chocolate bar.*) Look!

(*RACHEL looks longingly at it. HANS tempts her with chocolate.*)

HANS. Just walk over to the window and point to the man. That's all. (*Hans crosses to the window with her.*) That one? Or that one?

RACHEL. (*She struggles with decision, then lies.*) I don't know! I CAN'T TELL!!

HANS. (*Strikes her across the face.*) There are only five of them there. And you spoke directly to him. Now, which one was it?

RACHEL. I don't remember! They all ... look the same ... in prison clothes.

HANS. Why did you break the law?

RACHEL. I didn't know it was the law! And I won't do it again. Anyway, Herr Leutnant Schmidt, birthdays only come once a year!

HANS. (*Looks at her in astonishment.*) Madeleine, just how old are you?

RACHEL. Eleven.

HANS. Eleven! I wouldn't have believed you could be so naive. This is a waste of time! Now Madeleine Petit, never, NEVER, speak to strangers! A young girl of your age should know that. Why don't they teach you what's important at school? And if a prisoner ever tries to talk to you again, you are to come tell me at once. At once!

RACHEL. Yes, Herr Leutnant Schmidt.

HANS. Talking to a prisoner is treason. Punishable by death. Now, you don't want to be shot, do you?

RACHEL. No, Herr Leutnant Schmidt.

HANS. So, you must never break the law again.

RACHEL. Yes, Herr Leutnant Schmidt.
HANS. I'm talking to you just like a father.

(*RACHEL avoids looking at him. HANS pulls her face towards him.*)

HANS. AREN'T I!
RACHEL. (*Dully.*) Yes, Herr Leutnant Schmidt.
HANS. (*Gives Rachel her coat and helps her on with it.*) So, when you get home you can tell Frau Barbière and Fräulein Fleury that we had a nice little visit this afternoon and you learned an important lesson from Herr Leutnant Schmidt. (*HANS holds her by the shoulders until RACHEL nods.*) Now, run along. But remember, next time I won't be so lenient!

End of ACT I, Scene 5

ACT I

Scene 6

SCENE: *Madame Barbière's kitchen. June, 1944.*

AT RISE: *MARIE-THÉRÈSE BARBIÈRE and YVETTE REYNAUD are having coffee.*

YVETTE. And as long as I was coming I thought I'd bring you some of my almond cake.

MARIE-THÉRÈSE. I haven't had a piece of cake in two years! It tasted like real sugar.

YVETTE. (*Giggles.*) It was.

MARIE-THÉRÈSE. Real sugar?

YVETTE. Madame Barbière, you never mentioned that dear little girl was coming. Why didn't you say something to me? I could have given you lots of help.

MARIE-THÉRÈSE. I didn't know.

YVETTE. You didn't know? All the way from Marseilles and you didn't know?

MARIE-THÉRÈSE. Well, that is ... I found out ... just before. Family's family. You don't refuse.

YVETTE. Henri's cousin, isn't she?

MARIE-THÉRÈSE. Yes!

YVETTE. She doesn't look a bit like Henry. Not a bit.

MARIE-THÉRÈSE. No. She resembles the other side of the family. The Marseilles side.

YVETTE. Was Madeleine born there?

MARIE-THÉRÈSE. Yes. Why?

YVETTE. (*Smug.*) She doesn't have a Marseilles accent.

MARIE-THÉRÈSE. (*Pause.*) No. No, her mother insisted on the best convent schools, so she would speak a pure French. Thank you for the cake, Madame Reynaud. It's the little things that make wartime so hard. Who'd have thought I

would miss sugar in my coffee so much? Who'd
have thought the war would last so long?

YVETTE. There's plenty of sugar if you know
where to go.

MARIE-THÉRÈSE. Oh?

YVETTE. Down at the Town Hall, they have
it every day.

MARIE-THÉRÈSE. The Town Hall?

YVETTE. My dear Madame Barbière, you
don't think the Nazi officers pay attention to our
rationing, do you? They have sugar and real
chocolate and ... I suppose you heard about the
shooting in Le Puy?

MARIE-THÉRÈSE. No!

YVETTE. It's lucky I tell you the news. You
don't go out.

MARIE-THÉRÈSE. My arthritis -

YVETTE. Anyway, they caught a Jew hiding
in Monsieur Latour's barn.

MARIE-THÉRÈSE. Etienne?

YVETTE. Yes.

MARIE-THÉRÈSE. *(Fearfully.)* What
happened?

YVETTE. Well, Monsieur Latour swore he
didn't know anyone was hiding there. No one
believed that.

*(MARIE-THÉRÈSE is riveted. YVETTE sips
coffee before continuing.)*

YVETTE. So they shot them. And the dog. As an example.

MARIE-THÉRÈSE. An example!

YVETTE. There was a reward, too—six hundred francs. But Herr Leutnant Schmidt said we should do our duty without a reward.

MARIE-THÉRÈSE. (*Pensive.*) Yes. If we can.

YVETTE. I spoke right up. Right from the crowd. Money always helps, I told him.

MARIE-THÉRÈSE. (*Still shocked.*) They shot Etienne!

YVETTE. Can you imagine the danger for his neighbors?

MARIE-THÉRÈSE. Yes.

YVETTE. But I don't know why they shot the dog. Someone would have taken it in.

MARIE-THÉRÈSE. (*Ushering her out as fast as she can.*) Be careful crossing the road, Madame Reynaud. It may be June, but there's still patches of ice.

(*YVETTE exits. MARIE-THÉRÈSE closes the door, bolts it, and draws the lace curtains shut sharply. SHE opens the door to the armoire and turns on a radio. On the door is a map. SOUND: radio STATIC.*)

MARIE-THÉRÈSE. Suzanne! Madeleine!

SUZANNE. I'm coming.

(*SUZANNE runs in followed by Rachel.*)

MARIE-THÉRÈSE. I thought she wouldn't leave in time. Madeleine, stand here. Look out the window. Here. Through the crack in the curtains. If you see anyone, warn us.
RACHEL. All right.

(*SOUND: radio STATIC.*)

BRITISH RADIO VOICE. Good evening. This is the British Broadcasting Corporation. Key points in the German defense line in Italy have fallen. American troops have captured Valletri and Valmontone. Allied forces continue to push forward toward Rome ...
SUZANNE. (*She has marked the map with pins.*) Madame Barbière, look. The Allies are here. The Nazis still hold Rome, but by tomorrow, maybe-
RACHEL. Someone's coming.
MARIE-THÉRÈSE. Turn off the radio! Hide everything!

(*SUZANNE starts to close the armoire door.*)

MARIE-THÉRÈSE. No. No. (*Looks about frantically.*) Put it in the stove. Quickly.

(*SUZANNE hides radio in stove compartment.*)

MARIE-THÉRÈSE. Madeleine! Here!

(*MARIE-THÉRÈSE hands Rachel bowls, spoons,
    and a pot of soup to put on the table.*
*SOUND: FOOTSTEPS on the stone stairs.
    SUZANNE folds the map in her coat and drops
    it on the floor of the armoire. SHE closes it.*
SOUND: loud imperious KNOCK at the door.)

MARIE-THÉRÈSE. Who's there? (*Gestures to
Rachel to hurry.*)
HANS. Open up the door.
MARIE-THÉRÈSE. (*Sounding casual.*) Just
a moment. Just a moment.

(*MARIE-THÉRÈSE inspects to see if all signs are
    put away. SHE motions Rachel and Suzanne
    to the table. SUZANNE ladles soup so they can
    pretend to eat. MARIE-THÉRÈSE opens door.
    HANS enters.*)

SUZANNE. Herr Leutnant Schmidt!
HANS. I told you I would always knock first,
fräulein. Am I not a man of my word?

(*RACHEL starts to leave the table. HANS stops
    her.*)

HANS. There is no need to run away,
Madeleine Petit, unless you have done something
wrong.

MARIE-THÉRÈSE. (*Puts arm protectively around Rachel.*) She's still ashamed she caused you all that trouble, Herr Leutnant Schmidt. It won't happen again.

(*MARIE-THÉRÈSE guides Rachel away from Hans and towards her lacework. SHE helps her begin.*)

SUZANNE. You must excuse the table. We were just having supper. Are you hungry, Herr Leutnant Schmidt?

HANS. No. I have had my dinner. (*His eyes search the room*)

SUZANNE. (*Distracting him.*) But couldn't I tempt you with dessert—a piece of French cake and coffee?

HANS. (*Finds nothing amiss.*) Yes, if you made the cake.

SUZANNE. Me? Ah, no, no, no. It was made by Madame Reynaud. Have you met her, Herr Leutnant Schmidt?

HANS. Madame Reynaud? Reynaud? I don't think so.

SUZANNE. She's famous for her almond cake. It's her speciality.

HANS. Then I'll have some.

SUZANNE. (*Cuts piece and gives it to him.*) Here you are. Coffee?

HANS. (*Watching her move about.*) Yes. With lots of sugar.

SUZANNE. We have no sugar, Herr Leutnant Schmidt. Rationing.

HANS. Ah. Perhaps ... I could help you there. (*Takes a bite.*) Excellent. Excellent. (*Smacks his lips as he finishes the cake.*) Well, now, I must make it a point to meet this Madame Reynaud. (*HANS pulls out official paper.*) Someone reported that you were listening to a foreign radio station.

MARIE-THÉRÈSE. A radio? A foreign station? Why, you said yourself that was illegal.

HANS. I know what I said! Now, I won't sit at your table and then arrest you.

SUZANNE. (*Seizes the advantage.*) Oh ... you are not heartless, Herr Leutnant Schmidt. (*Sits beside him.*)

HANS. (*Doggedly.*) But someone reported hearing English voices in this house.

MARIE-THÉRÈSE. (*Musing.*) I always wanted a radio. The music would be such a comfort on a long winter's night. But there were never enough francs.

HANS. Explain that!

SUZANNE. Of course! Shall we tell him about our English lessons?

(*RACHEL looks uncertainly at Suzanne.*)

HANS. Why does she look so frightened?

SUZANNE. This! (*Leans over touching Hans gently as she removes whip. HE looks up at her*

eagerly.) Don't you know young girls prefer ...
sweets. Next time you come to see us ...

   HANS. I'll bring some. (*Annoyed.*) I have to
check this report.

   MARIE-THÉRÈSE. (*Chopping carrots by the
stove.*) Look for yourself.

(*HANS crosses to the armoire.*)

   SUZANNE. (*In pretty confusion.*) Oh dear!
My coat fell down! My scarf, my gloves ... all
over the floor! Excuse me.

(*SUZANNE scoops them up with the map and
   leaves the room. HANS investigates the
   armoire, knocks on the wall, overturns
   chairs.*
*SOUND: while HANS stalks the room in his
   JACKBOOTS, there is the counter-rhythm of
   Marie-Thérèse CHOPPING carrots and
   Rachel CLICKING the bobbins, as she makes
   lace.*)

   HANS. There's nothing here!
   SUZANNE. (*Returns and stands by the stove.*)
Of course not.

   HANS. Then explain.

   SUZANNE. Won't you sit down again?

(*HANS sits. SUZANNE signals Rachel with her
   eyes to listen closely.*)

"The quality of mercy is not strained,
It droppeth as the gentle rain from heaven
Upon the place beneath ..."
HANS. That's Shakespeare!
SUZANNE. A man who knows Shakespeare must be well educated.
HANS. I am!
SUZANNE. Then you must know it is always better to study poetry in the original. I try to teach some of the girls. Madeleine is learning. But the accent is ... very difficult. Particularly the sound of the "R". You see in French ...
HANS. I didn't come here for a French lesson! Let me hear the little girl.
SUZANNE. Madeleine, recite for Herr Leutnant Schmidt. (*Crosses to Rachel and whispers.*)
HANS. What are you whispering?
SUZANNE. (*With an angelic smile.*) Not to be afraid of you.
RACHEL. (*Recites the same passage, mispronouncing a few words.*)
"The quality of mercy is not strained,
It droppeth as the gentle rain from heaven
Upon the place beneath."

SUZANNE. (*Claps for her student.*) Herr Leutenant Schmidt! No applause? No thanks? When she tried so hard and did so well.

HANS. (*Applauds briefly.*) I see you are determined to teach me French manners.

SUZANNE. Good manners, Herr Leutnant Schmidt, are international.

HANS. (*Gets his coat. Holds Suzanne's hand lingeringly.*) I wish you would call me Hans.

SUZANNE. Hans.

HANS. You are ... very ... clever ... and very ... pretty.

SUZANNE. Thank you!

HANS. (*Still holding her hand.*) But I am not a fool! Auf Wiedersehen, fräulein, Frau Barbière, Madeleine. Another evening we will talk more. You will teach me the French "R". (*Exits.*)

RACHEL. Oh, Mademoiselle Fleury, I was so...

(*SUZANNE rushes to Rachel, puts finger to her lips.*)

SUZANNE. Sh-h. You were brave, little one. That's all that counts. (*Hugs her.*)

RACHEL. How did you know ... what to do?

SUZANNE. It's a lesson we don't teach in school; but it's as old as the Trojan War. When a man meets the enemy, he fights. When a woman meets the enemy, she flirts.

(*SOUND: MOTOR CAR.*)

MARIE-THÉRÈSE. Is he gone?
RACHEL. (*Looks out window.*) Yes.

(*The tension breaks. MARIE-THÉRÈSE and SUZANNE laugh together.*)

SUZANNE. When you said stove –
MARIE-THÉRÈSE. He never looked.

(*SOUND: the whistling of the beginning of a resistance song to the tune of "Auld Lang Syne." Their LAUGHTER halts. SUZANNE stands rigid. It is repeated. SUZANNE whistles the next phrase. SUZANNE checks the window and opens the door. JULIEN DELACOUR enters. HE is frenzied and worn.*)

SUZANNE. Julien!
JULIEN. (*Enters nervously. Hugs Suzanne.*) Thank God you're here. I was back this morning. But I had to wait until dark. Then I heard his car. I thought ... thought ... Thank God you're safe! What did he want?
MARIE-THÉRÈSE. A report. A radio. I told him I'd always wanted one.
JULIEN. Suzanne, I can't stay long. But I had to warn you. I– (*Exhaustion and hunger overtake him. SUZANNE and MARIE-THÉRÈSE help him to a chair.*)

MARIE-THÉRÈSE. Madeleine, some soup, some bread. Quickly! (*To Suzanne.*) ... He probably hasn't eaten.

(*RACHEL gets soup and bread.*)

SUZANNE. (*Holding him.*) You're shaking.
JULIEN. I'll be all right. I just need to eat. (*Devours a hunk of bread.*)
SUZANNE. Where were you?
JULIEN. Marseilles. (*HE eats more bread.*)
RACHEL. Marseilles! Please! Please tell me about Marseilles.
JULIEN. It's not for young ears.
RACHEL. Please! I must know. I must!
SUZANNE. Tell us, Julien.
JULIEN. You want the real news. Here! Read it in *our* paper, the *Maquisard.* (*Places resistance newspaper on table.*) They sent me down to write a story, conditions since the French surrender. (*Grips her arm.*) Suzanne, are you all right?
SUZANNE. I'm fine! What's wrong?

(*JULIEN eats hungrily.*)

MARIE-THÉRÈSE. He needs to eat, not talk,
JULIEN. No. No, I must talk. I must tell you.
RACHEL. Tell me about Marseilles. Please!
MARIE-THÉRÈSE. Her family was there. Henri's family.

JULIEN. There's no food in Marseilles. Except the black market. I saw a woman take off her wedding band to buy a slice of bacon. When I was in prison—

SUZANNE. Prison!

MARIE-THÉRÈSE.   (*Looking at him closely.*) I thought so.

SUZANNE. Julien, what happened? What happened to you?

JULIEN. They're arresting all the Jews in Marseilles.

(*RACHEL reacts.*)

JULIEN. They're going house to house, alley to alley, hunting them down. And they're arresting anyone who hides them. Anyone who gives them food, anyone who helps.

MARIE-THÉRÈSE. They shot someone in Le Puy. An example to the rest of us.

SUZANNE. Julien, why were you in prison?

JULIEN. I was cutting through an alleyway in Marseilles, when I say two soldiers beating up an old man. An old Jew with a beard. He was so weak, he hardly resisted. Then one of them set fire to his beard. I jumped the soldier from behind.

SUZANNE. Oh, Julien! Why?

JULIEN. I am who I am, Suzanne.

RACHEL. Did the old man get away?

JULIEN. That night he did. They beat me up instead, arrested me, dragged me off to prison. No food. No water. For four days. At the interrogation they accused me of being in the Maquis.

SUZANNE. What?

MARIE-THÉRÈSE. The Maquis?

JULIEN. A bluff to see if I'd break. They couldn't prove anything. But I found out about the ... the so-called labor camps ... in Poland, where they send–

MARIE-THÉRÈSE. Not in front of the child.

JULIEN. (*Points to paper.*) Then read it for yourselves later.

SUZANNE. (*Holds him, reassuring him.*) Julien, you're safe.

JULIEN. None of us is safe. Especially you.

SUZANNE. What do you mean?

JULIEN. Your last letter was in my wallet.

SUZANNE. My last letter? That was four months ago!

JULIEN. Yes.

SUZANNE. Why did you keep it?

JULIEN. Home! It reminded me of home. When they released me, they returned my belt, my watch, even all my money. But the letter was gone. I had to warn you, Suzanne. I had to warn you. (*Exhaustion takes over.*)

MARIE-THÉRÈSE. Let him sleep. Was *this* address on your letter?

SUZANNE. No.

MARIE-THÉRÈSE. Your last name?

SUZANNE. Just Suzanne.

MARIE-THÉRÈSE. Good! A man who's been in prison doesn't forget his fears so fast. Suzanne's a common name. Now, help me find a blanket for Julien. (*As SHE exits with Suzanne.*) Madeleine, cut some more bread and serve the soup. (*To Suzanne.*) Madeleine made the soup tonight all by herself.

(*RACHEL steals over to the paper and reads the lead article. SHE is visibly shocked.*)

RACHEL. No-o-o-o!!!

(*RACHEL runs out of the room choking back sobs. MARIE-THÉRÈSE and SUZANNE return. SUZANNE places blanket around Julien. MARIE-THÉRÈSE looks at table, irritated.*)

MARIE-THÉRÈSE. (*Calls.*) MADELEINE? MADELEINE?

(*RACHEL emerges, newspaper behind her.*)

MARIE-THÉRÈSE. I asked you to cut the bread and serve the soup! We're all hungry, and it's late.

RACHEL. I don't want any food.

MARIE-THÉRÈSE. (*The stress of the day shows.*) Other people live here besides you! There's no room for selfishness in this house.

RACHEL. (*Overreacting.*) Are you saying there's no room for me?

SUZANNE. (*Serving soup and slicing bread.*) Madame Barbière, come sit down.

MARIE-THÉRÈSE. I'm too old for all this trouble!

RACHEL. I didn't know ... you thought I was trouble! I thought— (*Runs out, dropping newspaper.*)

MARIE-THÉRÈSE. (*Tastes soup.*) Needs more salt! (*Adds it.*) She doesn't listen to me anymore.

SUZANNE. (*Picks up newspaper and reads.*) She was reading this.

MARIE-THÉRÈSE. When I was twelve, I did as I was told.

SUZANNE. (*Interrupts, reads aloud.*) "Mass murder report confirmed. Jews told they would be sent to live in a resettlement area are selected for hard labor. Or death. Either way, few survive. For them the only new country is heaven, not Poland. Families torn—"

MARIE-THÉRÈSE. (*Reads newspaper with increasing agitation.*) She shouldn't have seen this!

(*MARIE-THÉRÈSE exits abruptly. SUZANNE crosses to Julien, adjusts blanket around him,*

*sits beside him. MARIE-THÉRÈSE reenters
with RACHEL, who is wiping away tears.)*

MARIE-THÉRÈSE. We are all upset.
RACHEL. I'm sorry ... I ... I don't ... want ...
to be trouble for you. I'll go somepl–
MARIE-THÉRÈSE. Now don't be foolish!
Have some of your soup. It's very good. For a first
time.
RACHEL. *(Refusing it.)* People in Marseilles
are starving ... and ....
MARIE-THÉRÈSE. *(Sensibly.)* It doesn't help
them if you go hungry.
RACHEL. This war will never stop!
MARIE-THÉRÈSE. Yes, it will.
RACHEL. When?
MARIE-THÉRÈSE. You will be taller, that's
certain. And I'll be older, that's certain. But the
end will come. It always does. Until then, you
must have courage, little one. Courage!

*(RACHEL rests her head against Marie-Thérèse
and dozes. MARIE-THÉRÈSE, utterly
exhausted, closes her eyes. SUZANNE crosses
and reads the underground newspaper. SHE
is visibly upset. JULIEN opens his eyes and
watches her. SUZANNE sees he's awake,
crosses to him. THEY speak softly, so as not to
awaken the others.)*

SUZANNE. How do you know this is true? Murder? Children murdered? It can't be. It can't.

JULIEN. In ancient Greece they killed the messenger who brought news they didn't like.

SUZANNE. But Julien, how do you know?

JULIEN. I can't tell you that. One of the Maquis was there ... and saw enough.

SUZANNE. It wasn't you, was it? Was it?

JULIEN. (*Places fingers on her lips.*) A friend. But you've got to be careful. They have ... your letter. Your signature.

SUZANNE. There are hundred of Suzannes who write love letters in war time. They must have more to do than track each one of us down!

JULIEN. Listen to me, Suzanne! When Mussolini's men held Nice, they marched with mandolins. When the Nazis took over, the music stopped.

SUZANNE. (*Worried about him.*) You're not yourself. Stay here tonight.

JULIEN. I can't. War doesn't stop because the sun goes down.

SUZANNE. You need rest.

JULIEN. I'll sleep when it's over.

SUZANNE. (*In a mock embrace. Loudly.*) Goodnight. (*Whispers.*) What are my orders?

JULIEN. (*Kisses her on both cheeks. Loudly.*) Goodnight. (*Whispers.*) Pick up the boots from the cobbler. (*Places note in her hand.*)

SUZANNE. (*Whispers.*) Where do I bring them?

JULIEN. To the cafe. At five o'clock. (*Another mock embrace, whispers.*) If there's danger, drop your gloves! (*Loudly.*) Goodnight, darling. Goodnight, Madame Barbière.

(*SUZANNE looks at Marie-Thérèse with Rachel dozing by the fire.*)

SUZANNE. Look at them. Oh, Julien, the world could be so beautiful—

(*Impulsively, JULIEN kisses her.*)

SUZANNE. (*Flustered.*) We don't need to pretend now. They're both fast asleep.

JULIEN. I wasn't pretending. (*Exits.*)

MARIE-THÉRÈSE. (*Opens her eyes.*) I like your young man.

SUZANNE. What? Oh, oh yes.

MARIE-THÉRÈSE. When you get married, I will make the lace for your wedding dress.

SUZANNE. Madame Barbière, no one said ... anything about ...

MARIE-THÉRÈSE. Suzanne, my eyes can't see the thread as clearly as they used to. But they see other things—very clearly. He's part of the Maquis isn't he?

SUZANNE. (*Startled.*) Madame Barbière!

MARIE-THÉRÈSE. He's among friends. But there are many different ways to fight.

RACHEL. (*Wakes, stirs, half-asleep.*) Papa? Papa!

(*Automatically MARIE-THÉRÈSE comforts Rachel.*)

MARIE-THÉRÈSE. We each fight the war in our own way. (*Strokes Rachel's head gently.*) Go back to sleep, little one. (*With strong conviction.*) We each say, "No!" in our own way!

End of ACT I, Scene 6

ACT II

Scene 1

SCENE: Outdoor café. June, 1944.

AT RISE: SUZANNE is at a table waiting to meet Julien. SHE looks around anxiously and sees HANS enter. Quickly SHE drops her gloves.

SOUND: the CLOCK strikes five.

HANS. (*Sees Suzanne, crosses to table.*) Good evening, fräulein.
SUZANNE. Oh, Herr Leutnant Schmidt.

HANS. (*Picking up her gloves.*) You dropped these.

SUZANNE. I guess I did.

HANS. Why are you so formal tonight? I told you to call me Hans.

SUZANNE. I forgot ... Hans.

HANS. Are you waiting for someone?

SUZANNE. No.

HANS. Then I may join you. (*Sits before she answers.*) Tea or coffee?

SUZANNE. Coffee.

HANS. I'll get it. (*Exits.*)

(*SUZANNE quickly drops her gloves again. Looks about. Then powders her nose and looks in her mirror more carefully to see who is there. Sees JULIEN enter and SHE pointedly looks at her gloves. JULIEN exits.*)

HANS. (*Returns.*) Two coffees! (*HE sets coffees down. Sees gloves on floor.*) Is this a game? (*Picks up gloves and puts them in his pocket.*) They'll be safer here.

SUZANNE. No! I must have dropped them again. Please! (*Holds out her hand for her gloves.*)

HANS. (*Takes Suzanne's hand in his, smiling.*) I don't want to keep picking them up. After you and I have dinner, then I'll give them back to you.

SUZANNE. Dinner?

HANS. Your French rations are abominable. But I have sources. We'll eat at my hotel.

SUZANNE. (*Stalls.*) No, I really can't. Perhaps, some other time. But I have to correct papers this evening.

HANS. Then you certainly should eat dinner first.

SUZANNE. Oh, I couldn't. I'm not hungry yet.

HANS. I'm in no hurry. No hurry at all. Tell me about this village, St. Laurent des Pins.

SUZANNE. It began on the slope of that hill. Four hundred years ago. Some of the first stone houses are still standing. With the same families.

HANS. And the lace making? How old is that?

SUZANNE. Sixteenth century. I didn't know you were interested in all this, Hans.

HANS. Oh, I am. I am.

SUZANNE. Some of the women still pay homage to—

HANS. (*Interrupts. Takes her hand in his. Smiles.*) To the patron saint of lacemakers, Saint Francois Régis. You see I did my homework.

SUZANNE. Hans, you pronounced the name perfectly!

HANS. The French "R" can be mastered with a beautiful woman to inspire me. Suzanne—

SUZANNE. (*Nervously.*) They say the most beautiful lace is made right here, by hand, by women like Madame Barbière.

HANS. Interesting. (*Casually.*) And what do you know about Julien Delacour?

SUZANNE. (*Agitated.*) NOTHING!!!

HANS. We know you are—or were—his girl friend.

SUZANNE. A long time ago.

HANS. Good. I like the past tense. All we want to find out is where he is hiding.

SUZANNE. (*Rises angrily.*) Find out yourself.

HANS. (*Detains her.*) Suzanne, you are in no danger. Unless, you are lying.

SUZANNE. I don't know where he is. And I don't care. (*Takes out handkerchief and fakes crying.*)

HANS. A little bit of information now could protect you ... from further inquiries later. One word whispered, and I'll never say where I heard it. Painless.

SUZANNE. How should I know where he is! We had a fight. He left me. Months ago.

HANS. I see. Then next week you will do me the honor of coming to dinner.

SUZANNE. (*Stalls.*) Next week? I have to prepare exams!

HANS. You are conscientious. I admire that. But you must have some relaxation too. Why refuse an excellent dinner? Some women say I'm quite handsome.

SUZANNE. Oh, you are.

HANS. I'm glad you think so! Saturday, then. Whenever you're finished.

SUZANNE. But it might be too late.

HANS. I'll wait. I have the car if you would like a ride home now.

SUZANNE. No. No, thank you. I ... I need the fresh air.

HANS. "Fleury." That means flower, doesn't it?

SUZANNE. Yes. Why?

HANS. It suits you. A flower looks fragile, but it can be tough. We could use you in our New World. (*Exits.*)

(*SUZANNE's facade evaporates. SHE sits for a moment nervously. Then begins to gather her things. JULIEN comes from behind, puts a hand on her shoulder and pulls her back to her chair. They use the device of an embrace.*)

JULIEN. The boots?

SUZANNE. "The boots will be ready tomorrow." Julien, they're looking for you! How could you endanger the Maquis for one old man?

JULIEN. "The only thing necessary for the triumph of evil is for good men to do nothing." Edmund Burke.

SUZANNE. Go to Le Puy. But stay off the road.

JULIEN. Done.

SUZANNE. Now, go. The message must get there before noon.

JULIEN. It will. (*Exits.*)

(*SUZANNE waits a moment to make sure he's gone then adjusts make-up, hair.*
SOUND: offstage SCUFFLE.
HANS appears a second later.)

HANS. Ah, good! You're still here! I was already back in my hotel when I discovered I had these. (*Tosses the gloves on the table.*)

SUZANNE. My gloves!

HANS. I thought you'd want them.

SUZANNE. That was kind of you.

HANS. Also profitable.

(*SUZANNE looks puzzled.*)

HANS. I found the man I was looking for, Delacour.

SUZANNE. Julien!!!

HANS. He was just outside the café when we arrested him.

End of ACT II, Scene 1

ACT II

Scene 2

SCENE: Madame Barbière's kitchen. A half hour later.

AT RISE: RACHEL by the window, sees the first star.

RACHEL. Good night, Maman. (*Blows her a kiss, hears Marie-Thérèse coming and darts back to her lacework.*)

MARIE-THÉRÈSE. (*Enters limping and counting the pieces of lace.*) Two meters ... let's see ... at fifteen francs per centimeter ... that's ... hm-m-m ... Lucky for us the arthritis is in my legs and not my fingers, Madeleine!

RACHEL. Maybe we can sell some of my lace.

MARIE-THÉRÈSE. (*Crosses to inspect.*) Um-m-m. (*Holds up a piece.*) Um-m-m. Ah! Twist the thread around the pins this way. Watch. (*Demonstrates.*) Now you do it. (*Observes Rachel.*) That's right. (*Ruffling her hair.*) You can't rush fine lace, little one.

SUZANNE. (*Bursts in.*) They arrested Julien!

MARIE-THÉRÈSE. (*Crosses to comfort Suzanne.*) Maybe it's routine.

SUZANNE. He was on his way to Le Puy with a message.

MARIE-THÉRÈSE. Can you go instead?

SUZANNE. Schmidt's watching every move. If I'm not at work, he'll get suspicious. Oh, why was Julien so ... stupid?

MARIE-THÉRÈSE. Not stupid, Suzanne. Kind. I don't want to live in a world where kindness is called stupid.

SUZANNE. The message must get to Le Puy. Before noon tomorrow.

MARIE-THÉRÈSE. If my legs were better ...

RACHEL. I'll go!

MARIE-THÉRÈSE. It's twenty kilometers from here, little one.

RACHEL. I went with you last summer.

MARIE-THÉRÈSE. It's much too dangerous for you, Madeleine. Le Puy is full of Nazis.

RACHEL. (*Stubbornly.*) I know the way ...

MARIE-THÉRÈSE. No! This is no business for a little girl.

SUZANNE. That's the point. Who would guess?

MARIE-THÉRÈSE. I promised to take care of her, and I will.

RACHEL. But I want to go! And I'm twelve years old now!

MARIE-THÉRÈSE. What else could I expect in this house?

SUZANNE. Tomorrow's market day. You could start out at dawn. Can you whistle?

RACHEL. Yes.

SUZANNE. Then listen. (*SUZANNE whistles beginning of partisan song to tune of "AULD LANG SYNE."*) Repeat it.

(*RACHEL does.*)

SUZANNE. Our contact will be at a flower stand. Go there and whistle that song. When you hear him whistle the second part of the song, you repeat the first. Then buy some flowers - yellow flowers - whisper the message. No other song. No other person. No other color. Can you do that?

RACHEL. OF COURSE! What's the message?

SUZANNE. "The boots are ready."

RACHEL. I don't understand.

SUZANNE. Just deliver it. You can borrow my bicycle. But we should have a reason. A village girl wouldn't ride twenty kilometers to buy spring flowers.

RACHEL. (*Excited.*) I could sell some of Madame Barbière's lace. I've helped her before.

MARIE-THÉRÈSE. But not all by yourself.

SUZANNE. (*Excited.*) Yes, you could sell some lace. Let's fill the basket. Good thinking, Madeleine.

MARIE-THÉRÈSE. And what if someone asks her why I'm not there? Have you thought of that?

RACHEL. I'll say you're ill. Your leg is bad. It is!

MARIE-THÉRÈSE. She'll miss school. Her history test.

SUZANNE. Tomorrow, Madeleine will make history!

MARIE-THÉRÈSE. (*Holds Rachel.*) It is very dangerous. You don't know. You can't know.

RACHEL. Madame Barbière, you said we each must fight the war in our own way.

MARIE-THÉRÈSE. (*Relents.*) I did. But remember this.

MARIE-THÉRÈSE. What?

MARIE-THÉRÈSE. Many people have died for France. You, Madeleine, must live for France.

End of ACT II, Scene 2

ACT II

Scene 3

SCENE: *Early morning, the next day, Le Puy. Around the cobblestone square are outdoor stands and large café umbrellas to protect the fruits, vegetables and plants displayed. A lace store is at the edge. Just off the square is a narrow alley with a "No Parking" sign at the entrance. The sign is the traditional French red circular sign with white lettering.*

SOUND: CARTS *over cobblestones,* VENDORS' CRIES.

AT RISE: RACHEL *rides bicycle to the edge of the square, parks her bike hastily at the entrance to the alley and whistles the first few bars of the Resistance song. There is no response.*

MADAME REYNAUD *enters with a large straw market day basket.*

YVETTE. MADELEINE! Why aren't you in school? Is Madame Barbière here with you?

RACHEL. She's ill.

YVETTE. Ill! I just saw her yesterday, and she was well enough.

RACHEL. It's her leg, her arthritis.

YVETTE. Well, no wonder, keeping up with the likes of you! I warned her, young girls have to be watched every minute.

RACHEL. She sent me here.

YVETTE. You can't fool me!

RACHEL. She did. To deliver the lace.

YVETTE. Then where is it?

RACHEL. On ... on my bicycle.

YVETTE. On your bicycle? When did you get a bicycle? You're just enjoying yourself. I wouldn't keep the likes of you in my house, young lady.

RACHEL. (*Blurts out.*) I wouldn't stay in your old house. (*Quickly covers.*) Excuse me, Madame Reynaud. I—

YVETTE. Well!!! It's no concern of mine what happens to a girl like you. I don't go around interfering ... like some people. (*Exits.*)

(*RACHEL pretends to look at various stands, whistling the first few bars of the Resistance song over and over. Periodically, she looks back at her bike. At the furthest point from it, she sees Gérard, the gendarme, approach her bike to examine it. This time there is a response to her whistle. RACHEL is torn. SHE hears the refrain repeated. RACHEL whistles the first few bars. The refrain is repeated, and she locates the sound. RACHEL carefully selects a bouquet of flowers. SHE counts out the money to pay for them as the VENDOR gives her the flowers in newspaper.*)

RACHEL. (*Recites.*) "The boots are ready." (*SHE takes the bouquet and races to her bike, where GÉRARD is writing a ticket.*) No! No! Please.

GÉRARD. You're in a no parking zone, mademoiselle.

RACHEL. I'm sorry, officer.

GÉRARD. Is this your bicycle?

RACHEL. Yes.

GÉRARD. It's nice. Don't leave it like that. Someone could come and steal it.

RACHEL. Officer, do you have to write a ticket? I didn't know.

GÉRARD. You can read, can't you?

RACHEL. Of course.

GÉRARD. (*Points to the No Parking sign, and hands Rachel the ticket.*) It should be fifteen francs. I made it five. First offense.

RACHEL. (*Digs in her pocket and pays him.*) Thank you.

GÉRARD. (*Walks a few steps up the alley.*) Park it here.

RACHEL. But that's nearly the same place.

GÉRARD. But there's no sign.

(*YVETTE enters with HANS, who carries her basket.*)

HANS. Officer!

GÉRARD. (*Tips his hat.*) Good morning, Herr Leutnant Schmidt.

HANS. (*Curtly.*) Good morning. (*Stares at bike.*) Whose bicycle is that?

(*GÉRARD gestures to Rachel.*)

HANS. Arrest her!

GÉRARD. It was parked in the wrong place, that's all. I gave her a ticket.

HANS. And pocketed the fine? Arrest her?

GÉRARD. (*Stalls.*) Why?

HANS. The bicycle isn't hers. It's stolen.

YVETTE. I knew it! I knew it! Herr Leutnant Schmidt, it's just lucky I saw you.

GÉRARD. (*Disbelieving.*) Stolen? Are you sure? No. She doesn't look like a thief.

YVETTE. (*Smugly.*) Looks can deceive.

GÉRARD. (*Reluctantly, gently.*) Is it true? You can tell me. A pretty bicycle ... a pretty day ... you wanted to ride it around the square once. If you tell me now, it'll go easier for you.

RACHEL. No. It's not true.

GÉRARD. Ah, see. A mistake. All around. Bicycles look alike.

HANS. You call yourself a policeman? Afraid to arrest a little girl? No wonder France has lost the war!

(*HANS shoves him out of the way disgusted. GÉRARD and the bicycle both topple.*)

GÉRARD. (*Rising slowly.*) Some land, monsieur. Some battles. But not the war!

HANS. I'll deal with you later.

(*HANS turns to interrogate Rachel. As GÉRARD exits, HE glances back at Rachel.*)

HANS. Now, Madeleine, you will tell me why you have Fräulein's Fleury's bicycle.

YVETTE. Mademoiselle Fleury!

RACHEL. I ... I borrowed it.

YVETTE. And she told me she had to deliver lace for Madame Barbière.

RACHEL. The lace is right there!

HANS. (*Gives Yvette her basket.*) Don't let me detain you. Frau Reynaud.

YVETTE. Oh, Herr Leutnant Schmidt, I can wait. You said–

HANS. If she's who you think she is, Frau Reynaud, you'll get your reward. Now, leave us.

YVETTE. But–

HANS. LEAVE US!

YVETTE. I'm just going. (*Exits.*)

HANS. Now, Madeleine, we are going to talk, (*HANS leads her into alley. A shadowy face peers out from the plant and flower stand, sees that bicycle and flowers are strewn about, and puts up a sign that reads, "Closed.")* You see, Madeleine, I have a puzzle, A nice, neat puzzle, except there's a piece missing. And now you're going to help me find it.

RACHEL. Yes, Herr Leutnant Schmidt.

HANS. You're not her cousin, are you?

RACHEL. Whose?

HANS. Madame Barbière's.

RACHEL. Yes. Yes, I am!

HANS. You said before you were her husband's cousin. Which is it?

RACHEL. That's what I meant. Her husband's cousin!

HANS. (*Casually removes revolver.*) We will do whatever's necessary–to get the truth. Do you understand?

RACHEL. (*Concealing her fright.*) Yes.

HANS. Now, then, why did you steal the bicycle?

RACHEL. I didn't steal it. I ... I borrowed it. To deliver the lace.

HANS. Lace? (*Rips open package.*) LACE!

RACHEL. I told you.

HANS. Then why didn't you deliver it? Or sell it?

RACHEL. I just got here!

HANS. You had time to buy flowers. Who are the flowers for?

RACHEL. For Madame Barbière. She's sick. That's why I came.

HANS. What's your real name?

RACHEL. Madeleine Petit.

HANS. (*Consults notes again.*) Before you came to Auvergne, where were you?

RACHEL. Marseilles.

HANS. Did you always live there?

RACHEL. Yes.

HANS. And you were born there?

RACHEL. Just outside.

HANS. Frau Reynaud says you don't sound like someone from Marseilles.

RACHEL. Because my mother wanted me to speak French properly, without an accent.

HANS. Hand over your papers.

RACHEL. You already saw them.

HANS. (*Slaps her face.*) Don't play the fool. You see, we ferret you all out. No matter where you hide. We find you. (*Holds out his hand.*)

RACHEL. (*Hands papers over.*) I'm Madeleine Petit!!

(*HANS takes time to examine papers thoroughly.*
SOUND: the WHISTLE of the Resistance song.
RACHEL turns her head slightly to listen.
SOUND: the phrase is repeated.
HANS studies Rachel thoughtfully. SHE does not flinch.)

HANS. (*Slowly.*) Your papers ... are in order. So it should be no trouble for us to get more proof.

RACHEL. (*Startled.*) More!

HANS. (*Watches her.*) Someone who knew you in Marseilles, who can swear you are Madeleine Petit.

(*PÈRE ANTOINE and GÉRARD enter. GÉRARD points to bike. PÈRE ANTOINE crosses, looking for Rachel.*)

PÈRE ANTOINE. (*Puts bike upright.*) Madeleine! (*Crosses to them. GÉRARD exits.*) This child should be in school, Herr Leutnant Schmidt. Spring in this part of France. They won't stay inside. But I'll take her back.

HANS. That's not the issue!

PÈRE ANTOINE. (*Innocently.*) No?

HANS. No! (*Points to her.*) She's been accused. Is she a Jew?

RACHEL. (*Insists.*) I'm Madeleine Petit!

PÈRE ANTOINE. (*Laughs.*) Herr Leutnant Schmidt, we'd be insulted if this accusation weren't so absurd! Naturally, she's Madeleine Petit! Ever since I've known her, she's been Madeleine Petit.

HANS. Did you know her in Marseilles?

PÈRE ANTOINE. I brought her to St. Laurent myself. (*Puts arms protectively around Rachel.*)

HANS. This is no trifling matter.

PÈRE ANTOINE. I know.

HANS. You are telling the truth?

PÈRE ANTOINE. (*Indignant.*) It is my duty to do so.

HANS. Then you will vouch for her identity?

PÈRE ANTOINE. Certainly.

HANS. Perjury, Père Antoine, is punishable by death. Even for a priest.

PÈRE ANTOINE. Especially for a priest! We're taught not to lie in the eyes of God. As a priest I may think about heaven, but I'm in no rush to get there.

HANS. Do you swear that she is Madeleine Petit?

PÈRE ANTOINE. I know her by no other name.

HANS. You swear?

PÈRE ANTOINE. I swear.

HANS. A priest's word is sacred.

PÈRE ANTOINE. So they say. (*Pause.*)

HANS. I will accept it. (*Shakes hands with Père Antoine.*) Yvette Reynaud is a fool.

PÈRE ANTOINE. Ah! (*Gesture indicates HE agrees.*) There's one in every village.

HANS. (*A slight bow.*) My apologies, fräulein ... for the little ... inconvenience. (*Exits.*)

PÈRE ANTOINE. Madeleine, you must forgive stupidity.

RACHEL. No!

PÈRE ANTOINE. For your soul.

RACHEL. You can forgive stupidity for your soul. But I have to fight it, for my life!

End of ACT II, Scene 3

ACT II

Scene 4

SCENE: *Madame Barbière' s kitchen. August 25, 1944.*

AT RISE: *MARIE-THÉRÈSE, PÈRE ANTOINE, and SUZANNE study the map of France, which SUZANNE has marked to indicate the progress of the Allies and Axis forces. RACHEL is a lookout at the curtain.*

PÈRE ANTOINE. We're just outside of Paris.

SUZANNE. So close. So close. We need Julien.

MARIE-THÉRÈSE. It'll get worse before it gets better.

RACHEL. Why?

MARIE-THÉRÈSE. They're desperate. Madame Reynaud said the Nazis shot three hostages and left them dead in the street.

SUZANNE. We must get Julien out.

PÈRE ANTOINE. They've arrested the Bishop of Montauban.

MARIE-THÉRÈSE. The Bishop!

SUZANNE. Why?

PÈRE ANTOINE. For saying "all men are brothers, created by the same God." For saying that "the Anti-Semitic measures violated human dignity." It was a fine speech. There are many brave men in prison, Suzanne.

SUZANNE. Too many.

RACHEL. Is it time now?

MARIE-THÉRÈSE. Madeleine, you must learn some patience.

RACHEL. I can't stand waiting. I want to do something!

MARIE-THÉRÈSE. You did. Delivering that message to Le Puy was dangerous enough. Now, you stay home.

RACHEL. But I did more than that. I saved them too!

MARIE-THÉRÈSE. WHAT!

(SUZANNE signals Rachel to be quiet.)

MARIE-THÉRÈSE. What did you say?

RACHEL. Well, who'd suspect a girl just jumping rope. That was my idea.

MARIE-THÉRÈSE. SUZANNE! How could you let her?

RACHEL. Oh, I was only a lookout, Madame Barbière. They wouldn't let me pull out the train tracks.

MARIE-THÉRÈSE. I should think not!

RACHEL. We had to!

SUZANNE. A deportation train. Headed East.

RACHEL. We had to let them escape.

MARIE-THÉRÈSE. What if you'd been caught?

RACHEL. What if I did nothing!

MARIE-THÉRÈSE. To survive is enough! Suzanne, I want a live child at the end of the war, not a dead hero.

SUZANNE. Look at her carefully, Madame Barbière. *(Crosses to radio.)* She's young woman now. *(Turns radio on.)*

(RACHEL goes to lookout post.

SOUND: CHEERS, YELLING, CLAPPING. VOICES sing "La Marseillaise.")

MARIE-THÉRÈSE. La Marseillaise!!

(SOUND: Church BELLS ringing, HORNS honking.)

PÈRE ANTOINE. It must be!
SUZANNE. Sh-h-h.
BRITISH RADIO VOICE. An incredible sight, ladies and gentlemen. This morning French tanks entered Paris. Crowds line the street, waiting for the procession to pass. And when it does, Parisian women climb upon the tanks to kiss the soldiers and toss them flowers. On every balcony in Paris the tricolor has reappeared. Some are flags that have been hidden for years, some are rags tied together. But everywhere blue, white and red fly in the summer breeze. Never has the sun seemed brighter than today, August 25, 1944. All over the city there are signs, "Paris est libéré. Vive la France." Ladies and gentlemen, Paris is free!!

(THEY hug each other excitedly.)

RACHEL. Is the war over?
SUZANNE. Not quite.
RACHEL. But you said Paris is the heart of France.
SUZANNE. It is! Now we must free the rest of her!

MARIE-THÉRÈSE. And Julien. Before they kill him.

PÈRE ANTOINE. There's only one person who can walk in and out of prison at any hour without suspicion.

RACHEL. A guard?

PÈRE ANTOINE. A priest! I have an idea ...

End of ACT II, Scene 4

ACT II

Scene 5

SCENE: *A dark, tiny room in the detention prison at Le Puy. There are no furnishings. Only a tattered blanket on the floor. Late at night, August, 1944.*

AT RISE: *JULIEN is pacing the room.*

SOUND: *BOOTS walking; KEYS in a lock.*

PÈRE ANTOINE. (*To GUARD outside.*) Five minutes, Guard. No longer. (*Enters and says loudly.*) I've come to hear your confession, my son.

JULIEN. Père Antoine! What's happening? Why are you here?

PÈRE ANTOINE. (*Loudly.*) Kneel, my son, and pray for God's forgiveness. KNEEL!

(*JULIEN kneels and automatically recites a prayer.*)

PÈRE ANTOINE. Is he gone?

(*JULIEN nods.*)

PÈRE ANTOINE. I gave him a cigarette. Paris is liberated. (*Removes a hidden cassock.*)

JULIEN. We've been waiting two years to hear that! And I'm locked in here.

PÈRE ANTOINE. The door is never locked to a priest. Put this on. (*Helps him dress.*)

JULIEN. Why?

PÈRE ANTOINE. They need you out there. They need you more than they need me.

JULIEN. You can't take my place!

PÈRE ANTOINE. Don't argue. There's no time. I'm going to call for the guard. When I do, throw the blanket over me. They won't check till morning. By then you'll be far away from here. Take my hat.

JULIEN. You can't do this. They want to kill me.

PÈRE ANTOINE. They won't kill a priest! Go, Julien. Go! (*Calls loudly.*) Guard! I'm finished. (*PÉRE ANTOINE lies down and puts blanket over himself.*) Cover me.

(*JULIEN covers him, then pulls blanket off his
face for a split second.*)

JULIEN. Bless you, Père Antoine.

(*JULIEN again covers Père Antoine's face with
the blanket. JULIEN exits.*
SOUND: *BOOTS walking; KEYS in lock.*
LIGHTING: *Fades.*
SOUND: *In the dark, there is a GUN SHOT.
Silence. Then the rising sound of church
BELLS pealing. They signal peace.
Gradually they are mixed with "La
Marseillaise." The war is over.*)

End of ACT II, Scene 5

ACT II

Scene 6

SCENE: *Madame Barbière's kitchen, mid-May,
1945. It is decorated with miniature French
flags and tri-colored ribbon.*

AT RISE: *MARIE-THÉRÈSE and SUZANNE are
singing "La Marseillaise" as they work.*

THEY are preparing platters of cheese, French bread, and fruit. JULIEN is slicing sausage. RACHEL stares out the window, immobile.

MARIE-THÉRÈSE. She's been like that ever since the war ended. Standing by the window, hour after hour. For ten days. I don't know what to do.

(*SUZANNE crosses to Rachel, puts an arm around her.*)

RACHEL. They said they'd come! As soon as the war was over! They promised.

(*SUZANNE and JULIEN look at each other.*)

JULIEN. (*Crosses to Rachel.*) Some promises can't be kept.
RACHEL. I won't listen to you!
MARIE-THÉRÈSE. Madeleine, there are some things in life we must accept. Like Père Antoine's death last summer.
JULIEN. He said the plan was perfect. A change of clothes, and they'll never kill a priest.
MARIE-THÉRÈSE. He was always ... very persuasive.
JULIEN. He saved my life.
RACHEL. Mine, too. When Maman and Papa come, we have to tell them all about Père Antoine.

JULIEN. Madeleine, not everyone comes back.

RACHEL. (*Refuses to listen.*) They'll come! I know they will.

(*OTHERS look at one another helplessly.*)

MARIE-THÉRÈSE. (*Practical.*) Well, until then you'll stay right here. And there's a lot to do before the festival tonight!

(*RACHEL crosses to Marie-Thérèse.*
SOUND: CABRETTES. [A French instrument similar to the bagpipe.])

SUZANNE. The band! The first time since the war. Julien, did you ever see a more beautiful day?

JULIEN. (*Gazing at her.*) No. We'll dance the Bourée all night long.

SUZANNE. You too, Madeleine.

RACHEL. I don't know how.

JULIEN. Let's show her! (*HE grabs Suzanne and THEY show Rachel a few steps during the next few speeches.*)

JULIEN. Every Auvergnat dances the Bourée!

SUZANNE. It's a traditional dance.

JULIEN. And at the end the man kisses his partner on the cheek three times.

MARIE-THÉRÈSE. In my day, if the lady gave him a flower, then the gentleman knew she liked him.

RACHEL. Are you going to give Julien a flower?

SUZANNE. (*Embarrassed.*) Oh, Madeleine, I just pretended to be Julien's girl friend during the war to pass messages.

(*JULIEN is looking at her.*)

SUZANNE. We fooled everyone! (*To Marie-Thérèse.*) Even you.

MARIE-THÉRÈSE. Madeleine, go try on your party dress.

RACHEL. I already did.

MARIE-THÉRÈSE. (*Pushing Rachel out of the room.*) I need to check the length of the sleeves. (*RACHEL and MARIE-THÉRÈSE exit.*)

JULIEN. Is that true?

SUZANNE. What?

JULIEN. What you just said.

SUZANNE. It was their idea. The Maquis. Not yours.

JULIEN. That's how it started. That's not how it ended. Suzanne, I came back to marry you.

SUZANNE. That sounds like another order from the Maquis.

JULIEN. I thought about you, about us, the whole time. It's what kept me alive.

(SUZANNE waits for him to continue. JULIEN misinterprets her silence.)

JULIEN. But if your answer is no, I'll leave.

SUZANNE. Julien Delacour, how can I answer yes or no, when you didn't even ask me a question?

(SOUND: Bourée MUSIC continues. SUZANNE dances a step of the Bourée. JULIEN joins her. HE kisses her on the cheeks three times. SUZANNE smiles, hands Julien a flower.)

JULIEN. Suzanne Fleury ... will you ... please ... marry ... me?

SUZANNE. Oh, yes, Julien! Yes! *(In his arms.)* Oh, Julien, YES.

(THEY embrace.
SOUND: a KNOCK at the door. JULIEN ignores it.
SOUND: another KNOCK at the door. Reluctantly JULIEN goes to answer it. LÉON stands there, gaunt, grey haired. His clothes are army hospital surplus. HE is a shattered man, a shadow of himself.)

LÉON. I'm looking for Madeleine Petit. They said Madame Barbière's house.

(*JULIEN hesitates, looking at Léon's appearance.*)

LÉON. I'm her father.
SUZANNE. Come in!

(*LÉON enters.*)

SUZANNE. (*To Julien.*) Go get Madeleine.

(*JULIEN exits.*)

SUZANNE. I'm Suzanne Fleury, her teacher. (*THEY shake hands.*) Please sit down.

(*LÉON sits.*)

SUZANNE. She has been waiting by the window, hoping her maman and papa would come.
LÉON. I've come alone.

(*MARIE-THÉRÈSE enters nervously with her hands firmly on Rachel's shoulders. As RACHEL enters, SHE stops, stares, stunned by Léon's altered appearance. SUZANNE exits.*)

RACHEL. Papa? (*Pulls away from MARIE-THÉRÈSE and crosses slowly to him. There is a long look.*) Papa! (*THEY embrace.*) I knew you'd come. They said—but I knew you'd come. (*Runs to the door.*) Maman.

LÉON. She's not there.

RACHEL. Where is she?

(*LÉON doesn't answer.*)

RACHEL. Papa, where is she?

(*LÉON shakes his head.*)

RACHEL. Papa! Tell me!

LÉON. Typhus. She died of typhus in the camp.

RACHEL. No! Not Maman! NOT MAMAN. Maybe she escaped. Maybe—

LÉON. You can't understand. You weren't there. There was only one escape.

RACHEL. I made a lace tablecloth just for her. And every evening as soon as the first star appeared, I said goodnight. Just the way we said we would. (*Turns on him violently. All the pent up rage and fear pours out.*) She can't be dead. She can't be. Why didn't you stop them?

(*MARIE-THÉRÈSE pulls her away.*)

RACHEL. I hate them. I HATE THEM! I HATE THEM!

LÉON. (*Drained.*) Hating won't bring her back.

MARIE-THÉRÈSE. But it helps. (*Gathers Rachel in her arms.*) I'm Madame Barbière. (*RACHEL sobs. To Léon.*) When a river is swollen, it floods. Let her cry, monsieur, let her cry. Nature knows more than we do about healing.

LÉON. (*Far away.*) I ... can't ... cry.

(*SUZANNE and JULIEN have reentered.*)

SUZANNE. (*To Léon.*) This is Julien Delacour, my fiancé. (*THEY shake hands.*)

MARIE-THÉRÈSE. Ah! Fiancé! Did you hear that, Madeleine?

(*There's a little nod amidst the sobs.*)

RACHEL. (*Raising her head.*) Papa, where were you?

LÉON. Many places.

SUZANNE. Tell her the truth.

LÉON. I ... I can't.

RACHEL. You were in one of those camps, weren't you?

(LÉON nods.)

RACHEL. In Poland?

LÉON. Poland, Germany. After awhile it doesn't matter. They can only kill you once, (*To Rachel.*) But you still have one of us left.

RACHEL. (*Crosses to him slowly.*) So do you, Papa. So do you. (*Looking at him.*) You look, so ... so ... so different?

LÉON. The Americans sent me to a hospital to fatten me up!

MARIE-THÉRÈSE. (*Drily, bring him some food.*) They didn't finish.

RACHEL. What about Maman?

LÉON. Too late. (*Touches her face.*) You're so healthy! Madame Barbière, you've given me my daughter! A reason to hope.

MARIE-THÉRÈSE. War is strange, monsieur. I could say the same.

LÉON. How can I thank you?

MARIE-THÉRÈSE. Don't take her away so soon. Stay with us ... a few days.

LÉON. I owe you too much already.

MARIE-THÉRÈSE. We'll talk about that later. Later. Right now you need mountain air and rest. And more than a day of it. Even with our famous cabbage soup, I can't work miracles.

LÉON. (*Gazing at Rachel.*) I think you already have.

RACHEL. Papa, stay. Until you're stronger.

SUZANNE. (*Softly to Léon.*) It would give her some time, too.

RACHEL. Please, Papa, stay.

LÉON. All right, Rachel. All right.

MARIE-THÉRÈSE, SUZANNE, & JULIEN. (*Together.*) RACHEL?

LÉON. (*To Rachel.*) I haven't said it aloud since the night you left.

RACHEL. Neither have I, Papa.

LÉON. Two and a half years.

RACHEL. (*A slow realization.*) Madame Barbière, they wouldn't really have shot you, would they?

(*SHE doesn't answer.*)

RACHEL. WOULD THEY?

MARIE-THÉRÈSE. I couldn't leave you out in the snow.

LÉON. (*Seated. Far away.*) Others did.

RACHEL. Papa? (*Touches his face gently.*) You sound so ... so far away.

LÉON. (*A trace of tears beginning in his voice.*) Rachel. My dearest Rachel. I'm coming home ... slowly.

(*LÉON is seated, his head down. RACHEL stands behind him, her arms on his.*)

RACHEL. It's over, Papa. The war's over. We can stop hiding! I can have my name back. My own name. RACHEL SIMON!

THE END

PRODUCTION NOTE

HYMN

The hymn used by Père Antoine in Act I, Scene 2 is from the liturgy of Good Friday. It describes the crucified Christ speaking to his "people." The suggestion to use this hymn was made by Father Frederick Tollini, Department of Theatre Arts and Dance, Santa Clara University, California. It was chosen to suit the emotions and situation of the scene. "The priest in the play could see the murdered Jew as a 'Christ figure' or conversely that Christ is made 'present today' in the figure of the Jew killed by the powers that are in control."

BOURÉE MUSIC

Appropriate music for this traditional dance can be found on recordings of French traditional music.

Recommended sources:

French Traditional Music from the Limousin
Shanachie Record Corporation
Dalebrook Park
Ho-Hokus, NJ 07423
LOJAI
21008 Shanachie, 1986
BOURÉE DE SAINT GENEST

Chez Nous En France: L'Auvergne, Vol: 1,
L'Aubrac
   AFA
   5019DA37
   FNAC
   Forum Des Halles
   75001 Paris, France
   Disque 2-Face C
   any one of the bourées 7,11,12
   Face D-any one of the bourées 2,4, 6, 8, 9

COSTUME PLOT

NOTE: The early-to-mid 1940's was a period of austerity, of "make-do and mend." (The one exception was women's hats!) During the war there was rationing of all kinds, including clothing. The attire indicated below is of the early 1940's; but it is perfectly plausible, particularly in the French countryside, that the clothing would be from an earlier period.

Period hairstyles should be followed.

PAULINE
ACT I, Scene 1
Ginger crepe dress, jewel neck, square shoulders, skirt just below knee
White lace shawl (worn for Sabbath blessing)
Rayon Stockings
Brown suede platform shoes

LÉON
ACT I, Scene 1
Dark brown, wool, 3-button sack suit with wide lapels
Matching vest with pocket for watch
White shirt
Conservative wide, pointed tie
Brown socks
Dark brown leather oxford shoes
Black yarmulke (worn for Sabbath blessing)

ACT II, Scene 6
Grey V-necked cardigan sweater (oversized)
Grey twill trousers (baggy)
Blue flannel shirt
Dark socks
Dark, shabby work shoes
N.B. In this scene he appears gaunt, and his hair is grey. He is wearing hospital surplus clothing.

RACHEL
ACT I, Scene 1
Torn and dirtied school uniform (Grey smock with buttons down the back, Peter Pan collar, sash at waist, skirt below knees)
Black knee socks
Black round-toes oxford shoes
Change to: Hand-smocked blue-and-white checked dress, with white collar, ties in back with a bow, skirt above knee
White anklet socks
Black flat shoes with strap, round-toed
Navy wool coat, princess style
Navy beret
Navy leather gloves
Small navy purse

ACT I, Scene 2
Same as in the end of ACT I, Scene 1
ACT I, Scene 3
Same as in the end of ACT I, Scene 1

ACT I, Scene 4

School uniform (Black, long-sleeved, button-down blouse, Peter Pan collar with black wool skirt with slight flare, mid-calf.)

Black wool lisle stockings

Coat, beret, and gloves (from I, 1)

Black, round-toed oxford shoes (from I, 1)

ACT I, Scene 5

School uniform, stockings, (from I, 4)

Coat and beret and oxford shoes (from I, 1)

Red, hand-knitted, wool scarf and mittens

ACT I, Scene 6

Hand-smocked berry-red print dress, short sleeved, skirt above knees

White pinafore

White anklets and black flat shoes with strap, round-toes (from I, 1)

ACT II, Scene 2

White blouse, short sleeved, with Peter Pan collar

Navy flared skirt above knees

Navy purse, knee-length socks, dark oxford shoes (from I, 1)

ACT II, Scene 3

Same as in the previous scene

ACT II, Scene 4

White blouse (from II, 2)

Short, full, dark print cotton skirt, knee length

Cork sandals

ACT II, Scene 6
White peasant blouse with puffed sleeves,
trimmed in lace
    Short full blue print cotton skirt, knee length
    Sandals (from II, 4)

PÈRE ANTOINE
(All scenes)
Black cassock
Black round brimmed hat
Black shoes

GÉRARD
(All scenes)
Traditional gendarme's uniform: dark navy
jacket, trousers, cape, cap
    White gloves
    Dark shoes

HANS
(All scenes)
Khaki Nazi Lt. uniform: jacket, trousers, cap,
uniform shirt and tie, revolver, holster, whip,
black jackboots
    Khaki overcoat (used in I, 4 only)

YVETTE
ACT I, Scene 2
Heather, wool tweed travelling suit with
square shoulders, V-neck, nipped in waist, skirt
just below knees

Tiny saucer hat with veil, worn at a tilt
Matching purse, gloves and platform shoes
Neutral rayon stockings
ACT I, Scene 6
Blue/green print dress, jewel neck, short-sleeved, square shoulders, skirt just below knees
Study, low-heeled black pumps with straps
Neutral stockings (from I, 2)
Jewelry
Light blue, torso-length flared jacket
Headscarf
ACT II, Scene 3
Yellow/beige/white flowered print dress with square shoulders, V-neck, skirt just below knees
Large white hat
Beige shawl or cardigan
Beige open-toed platform shoes with ankle straps
Neutral stockings (from I, 2)
Beige handbag
White summer jewelry

MARIE-THÉRÈSE
ACT I, Scene 3
Black, long-sleeved dress, rather shapeless and much longer than the fashion
Maroon cardigan
Black Lisle stockings
Black lace-up shoes with slight heel, comfortable, sturdy
Chef's apron

ACT I, Scene 6
Same as in previous scene except black felt
slippers instead of shoes
ACT II, Scene 2
Black shirtwaist dress, short-sleeved, brooch
at throat, skirt a few inches below the knees
Black lisle stockings (from I, 3)
Black felt slippers (from I, 6)
Chef's apron (different)
ACT II, Scene 4
Dress same as in previous scene
Stockings and sturdy black shoes (from I, 3)
ACT II, Scene 6
Same as in previous scene but with lace collar

SUZANNE
ACT I, Scene 4
Black wool sweater set
Grey, wool tweed skirt with kick pleat, just
below knees
Black, grey and red silk scarf
Grey wool coat with tie belt
Matching wool scarf, hat, and gloves
Rayon stockings
Black ankle boots
ACT I, Scene 6
Cream-colored tailored blouse, V-neck
Camel colored skirt with kick pleat, just below
knees
Stockings (from I, 4)
Dark low-heeled pumps with strap

ACT II, Scene 1
Dark, flowered print dress, V-neck, framed in lace, square shouldered, flared skirt, just below knees
Torso length jacket matching one color in dress
Rayon stockings and pumps from (I. 6)
Matching gloves and handbag
Headscarf
ACT II, Scene 2
Same as previous scene
ACT II, Scene 4
White print summer dress, belted, short-sleeved, flared skirt, just below knees
Cork platform sandals
ACT II, Scene 6
White lace blouse with cap sleeves
Red skirt, short, full
Cork sandals (from II, 2)

JULIEN
ACT I, Scene 4
Black ribbed-wool sweater, round neck
Grey trousers
Dark wool-lined leather jacket with wing collar (aviator)
Dark wool gloves
Black beret
Dark heavy work shoes
Black socks
Grey wool muffler

ACT I, Scene 6
Soiled white shirt
Torn dark trousers
Dark shoes and socks (from I, 4)
Burgundy, pullover, cableknit sweater
Beret (from I, 4)
ACT II, Scene 1
White shirt, open at throat
Beige corduroy jacket
Dark brown trousers
Dark, heavy shoes and socks (from I, 4)
ACT II, Scene 5
White shirt, soiled
Dark brown trousers, soiled
Dark, heavy shoes and socks (from I, 4)
Black priest's cassock
ACT II, Scene 6
Navy, summer jacket, 3-button
White shirt
Red-and-navy striped tie
Light blue trousers
Dark socks
Dark shoes

PROPERTY PLOT

All properties appropriate to period 1942-45, France.

ACT I, Scene 1: Hotel Room
Small hotel table covered with white linen cloth
3 chairs, cane, straight back
China soup tureen, patterned; silver ladle
Matching china soup bowls
3 soup spoons
3 white linen napkins
Black leather schoolbag. This is a briefcase with 2 pouch pockets and 2 buckles in front, fastened by shoulder straps and carried on the back
White handkerchief (RACHEL)
Assorted cotton rags and metal basin of water (LÉON)
Small hotel desk with drawer
Ink pad
Carte D'Idéntité (identity card) 9" x 6 3/4". When folded becomes 4 1/2" x 6 3/4". Headshot Photo inside, upper right-hand corner. Thumb print on inside, right-hand side of the lower portion of the card
Envelope with French francs
Envelope with birth certificate and food ration card
Small, dark leather suitcase (RACHEL)

Navy winter coat and beret (PAULINE brings on for RACHEL)

3 silver candle holders with white candles and matches, practical on silver tray

Silver wine goblet

White shawl (PAULINE)

Black yarmulke (LÉON)

ACT I, Scene 2: Train Carriage

French newspaper (Yvette)

Book (PÈRE ANTOINE) possibly by Condorcet, 18th century French philosopher

Bible, leatherbound, worn (PÈRE ANTOINE.)

Identity cards (see above) (PÈRE ANTOINE, YVETTE, RACHEL)

Train ticket (RACHEL)

Luggage on carriage rack: (PÈRE ANTOINE's battered leather bag, YVETTE's suitcase and hat box, RACHEL's small suitcase)

Small, navy, child's purse (RACHEL)

Shoulderbag (YVETTE)

ACT I, Scene 3: Madame Barbière's kitchen

Black, cast iron, wood-burning cooking stove with either a) separate plate warmer compartment or b) the kind with wells. In the case of the latter the wells connect to the wood firebox but can be closed off by damper. One well would hold soup pot, the other would have a griddle. The opening must be large enough to hold a homemade, small, wood rectangular box-style radio.

Lace curtains at the window

Iron cooking pot with metal handle with cabbage soup on stove

Ladle

French soup bowl with handles

Flatware soup spoon

Framed, ornamental lace patterns on wall (can be done scenically)

Cooking pots and utensils on wall by stove (can be done scenically)

Coat (RACHEL)

Table with 2 chairs (can be from I, 1)

1 comfortable chair by stove with small footstool

Pillow lace cushion with bobbins

Armoire (practical)

ACT I, Scene 4: School

Wooden desk

Straightback, squareseat wood chair

A plant

School text books

School papers

School bag, winter coat and beret (RACHEL, from I, 1)

School roster book (a thin, large booklet approximately 10" x 14" when closed. The cover is brownish-beige, like wrapping paper. It has the following information: Académie de St. Laurent

des Pins, Départment de Haute Loire, Ecole de
Primaire, Année Scolaire 1942-43)
     Small leather notebook (HANS)
     Whip (HANS)

ACT I. Scene 5: Town Hall
Nazi flag
Stool or wooden chair
Desk with drawer (can be from I, 1 or I, 4)
Large chocolate bar in desk drawer
Wristwatch (HANS)
Winter coat, beret (RACHEL, From I. 1)
Red scarf and mittens (RACHEL)

ACT I. Scene 6: Madame Barbière's kitchen
Cast iron stove (from I. 3)
Soup pot with ladle (from I, 3)
Framed ornamental lace (from I, 3)
Lace curtains (from I, 3)
Table & 3 chairs (from I, 3)
Armoire (from I, 3)
Inside armoire: map of Europe 1944, marked
with pins, removable, foldable. Suzanne's coat
with pockets, scarf, gloves. Small homemade
radio, black formica, 8 1/2" x 8 1/2", round
speaker center, 2 knobs, and dial below
     Comfortable chair with footstool (from I, 3)

Cake[*] on serving plate with cake knife
3 cake plates with cake forks
3 demitasse cups and saucers
Coffee pot
4 soup bowls and 4 soup spoons
French bread in chunks in basket
Knife, cutting board, raw carrots
Soup pot on stove (from I, 3)
Soup tureen
French underground newspaper *The Maquisard* (JULIEN)
Whip (HANS)
Folded piece of paper (JULIEN)
Pillow lace cushion with bobbins (MARIE-THÉRÈSE, from I, 3)
Pillow lace cushion with bobbins (RACHEL)
Wool blanket (MARIE-THÉRÈSE)

ACT II, Scene 1: Cafe
Café table with 2 chairs
Gloves (SUZANNE)
2 demitasse cups and saucers (from I, 5)
Pocketbook with handkerchief, makeup and mirror inside (SUZANNE)

---

[*] The almond cake is a small round cake 8" in diameter made with flour, sugar, eggs, almond paste and a frangipane filling. The texture is similar to a pound cake. The top of the cake is sugared or glazed and could have almonds.

ACT II, Scene 2: Madame Barbière's kitchen
Cast iron stove, cooking pots and utensils, framed lace patterns, table & chairs, lace curtains, comfortable chair and footstool, armoire (from I, 3)

Pillow lace cushion with bobbins (RACHEL, from I, 6)

Pieces of lace (MARIE-THÉRÈSE)

Brown wrapping paper and string

ACT II, Scene 3: Market
Bicycle with basket that has wrapped package of lace (RACHEL)

Straw market basket (YVETTE)

No Parking sign, traditional French red circular sign with white lettering (can be done scenically)

Flower stalls with a variety of flowers, among them yellow (can be done scenically)

Bouquet of yellow flowers (RACHEL)

Newspaper to wrap flowers (VENDOR)

French coins (RACHEL)

Traffic violation ticket and policeman's pen (GÉRARD)

Purse with identity card (RACHEL)

Revolver (HANS)

ACT II, Scene 4: Madame Barbière's kitchen
Cast iron stove, cooking pots and utensils, framed lace patterns, table & chairs, lace curtains, comfortable chair and footstool, armoire (from I, 3)
Map and radio inside armoire (from I, 6)

ACT II, Scene 5: Cell
Tattered, soiled blanket
Black priest's cassock (PÈRE ANTOINE for JULIEN)

ACT II, Scene 6: Madame Barbière's kitchen
Cast iron stove, cooking pots and utensils, framed lace patterns, table & chairs, lace curtains, comfortable chair and footstool, armoire (from I, 3)
Tri-colored decorative ribbon
Small French flags
Platter of cheese (bleu d'Auvergne, similar to blue cheese)
Basket of French bread
Platter of fruit
A sausage and meat knife and meat platter
A vase of wild daffodils on table

For a happy opening night
and
Hungry people anytime

POTÉE DE MADAME BARBIÈRE
Serves 4–6

Ingredients:

1/2 head cabbage,	1/2 cup parsley; 1 bay leaf
1 large onion studded with cloves	1/2 t. sage; 1/2 t. thyme
2 turnips, 3 carrots, 3 potatoes (peeled, cut into small chunks),	3T olive oil,
4 cups beef stock	salt and pepper to taste,
1 1/2 lbs cooked ham or salt pork cut into small pieces.	*optional:* 1 clove garlic minced

Directions:

Break cabbage up. Put in large pot. Cover with beef stock. Add other ingredients. Bring to boil. Reduce to simmer. Cook slowly for 1 1/2 hours.

This is a hearty soup best served with French bread. With salad, it's a meal!

REMEMBER MY NAME

AREA I   Basement hotel room I/1
          School I/4
          Cafe II/1

AREA II   Market II/3

AREA III Train Carriage I/2
          Town Hall I/5
          Cell II/5

AREA IV   Kitchen I/3, I/6, II/2, II/4, II/6

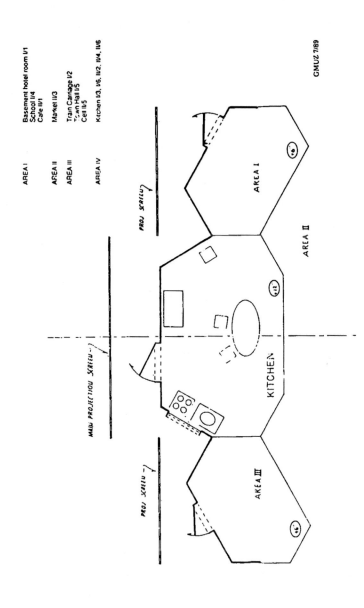

GMUZ 7/89